ILLUSTRATING SPAIN
in the US

Editor and curator: **ANA MERINO**
Project coordinator: **ERNESTO CORO**
Translator: **MARTA GONZÁLEZ-CUTRE**
Editorial Assistance: **CONRAD GROTH**
Designer: **KEELI McCARTHY**
Associate Publisher: **ERIC REYNOLDS**
Publisher: **GARY GROTH**

Cover by **SONIA PULIDO**

This project was commissioned by the Cultural Office of the Embassy of Spain and the Spain-USA Foundation through its SPAIN arts & culture program (www.spainculture.us).

  SPAIN / USA /
/ Foundation /

Fantagraphics Books, Inc.
7563 Lake City Way NE
Seattle, WA 98115

www.fantagraphics.com
facebook.com/fantagraphics
@fantagraphics

ISBN: 978-1-68396-508-4
Library of Congress Control Number: 2021940044
First Fantagraphics Books edition: January 2022
Printed in China

Illustrating
Spain in the US

Contents

Introduction

Ana Merino

PROFESSOR OF SPANISH CREATIVE WRITING AND CULTURAL STUDIES, UNIVERSITY OF IOWA

SPAIN HAS BEEN AN ESSENTIAL seedbed in the substratum of American history and culture. From Spain's missionary efforts in the 16th century to the Revolutionary War to the heyday of Hollywood and beyond, Spaniards have played a significant role in the history of the United States. Commissioned by the Cultural Office of the Embassy of Spain in Washington, D.C., this project brings together some of Spain's most celebrated cartoonists and scholars to spark a creative dialogue about Spain's legacy in the US.

Sergio García achieves this with his stunning map of the Viceroyalty of New Spain, colored by Lola Moral, which explores San Agustín, Las Misiones and the Camino Real. Rayco Pulido brings the historical figure of Bernardo de Gálvez to life, illuminating the key — but often overlooked — role he played in the American War of Independence. Through their expressive linework, Ana Penyas and Seisdedos recreate the lost generations of Spanish immigrants that found a new home in the US, while never forgetting their origins. Anapurna reminds us of the power of Hispanism with an illustrated poem that evokes the poetics of the diaspora. Mireia Pérez celebrates the Spanish scientists who made great achievements on American soil and immerses herself in their imaginative minds. Carla Berrocal applauds the passionate soul of Spaniards in Hollywood. Guided by a magpie and three cats escaped from a Goya painting, Max leads us through the labyrinthine history of Spanish art collecting in the United States. In addition, Sonia Pulido opens the door to these perspectives with a front cover depicting a symbolic representation of some of the characters that were touched by the experience of this dynamic history between both countries. In a playful way, Sonia combines the Spanish and American flags, showing the colorful and vital human energies within them and the future essence of the entrepreneurial illusion of the Spanish diaspora.

The versatility of the comics medium allows for a nuanced representation of this living diaspora of Spanish men and women who have been and continue to be intertwined with the American experience. Historians and scholars J. Michael Francis, Eduardo Garrigues, James Fernández, Luis Argeo, Lucía Cotarelo Esteban, Juan Pimentel, Estrella de Diego and María Dolores Jiménez-Blanco act as the interlocutors, explaining these complicated histories to cartoonists and inspiring their comics creations.

Illustrating Spain in the US thus combines the graphic expressiveness of comic art with the illuminating perspective of scholarly essays. Informed by academic research, these graphic stories demonstrate Spain's place in the imagination of the United States even before the country's very founding. This Spanish energy that so fascinates Americans, marked by a vibrant passion and creativity, was present from the very first Spanish immigrants and has continued in successive generations, from the actors who have graced the screen, the artists and academics who have created vital works and the scientists who have made — and continue to make — astonishing advances.

MISSIONS AND
THE CAMINO REAL

Missions and the Camino Real in Spain's North American Frontier

J. Michael Francis

HOUGH FAMILY CHAIR OF FLORIDA STUDIES, PROFESSOR OF HISTORY, UNIVERSITY OF SOUTH FLORIDA, ST. PETERSBURG CAMPUS

THROUGHOUT SPANISH AMERICA, the mission served as a critical frontier institution, part of a low-cost collaborative effort between the Crown and the clergy to expand Spain's presence across the continent, challenge imperial rivalries, increase economic development, colonize native populations and convert them to Christianity. It was an ambitious enterprise, one that has left a complex legacy. On one hand, missions were places of enduring alliances, peaceful cultural exchange, economic productivity and religious transformation. At times, missions also became centers of violent clashes, epidemic outbreaks and other hardships. Dozens of friars lost their lives at the hands of those they sought to convert, and thousands of Native Americans perished from disease and excessive labor demands. It is not surprising that the legacy of the mission system continues to inspire public imagination, attract tourists and generate heated debate.

Beginning in the 16th century, Jesuit and Franciscan friars established a constellation of Catholic missions in North America, stretching from the Chesapeake Bay to the Florida Keys and eventually across the continent to California. Some of these missions were short-lived, enduring just months, while others permanently transformed the landscape, leaving impressive structures that have survived to the present.

While the earliest missionary efforts in Florida date back to the early decades of the 16th century, it was not until the 1560s that Spain established a permanent presence in the region. On March 15, 1565, Pedro Menéndez de Avilés signed a detailed contract with Spain's King Philip II, outlining the terms of an ambitious colonization enterprise to North America. Among the many obligations outlined in Menéndez's contract was a mandate to evangelize Florida's Native population. To that end, Menéndez agreed to transport and provision four Jesuits and 12 additional friars to lead the evangelization efforts.

Six months later, Menéndez and 800 soldiers and settlers landed on the north coast of Florida. There, they founded the garrison town of St. Augustine, the oldest permanently occupied European settlement in the continental United States. The following year, Menéndez petitioned Francisco Borja, the Jesuit General in Rome, to dispatch a group of Jesuits to Florida to lead the evangelization efforts. Borja agreed, and in September 1566 the first three Jesuits reached the province. Between 1567 and 1572, fewer than a dozen Jesuits established a string of missions, including missions at Tocobaga (present-day Tampa Bay) and Tequesta (present-day Miami). Native hostility to Jesuit conversion efforts combined with a lack of support from Spanish officials led to the rapid abandonment of Florida's Jesuit missions. In a final effort to revitalize their missionary efforts, eight Jesuits journeyed north to the Chesapeake Bay, where they established a fledgling mission at Jacán. It was not long before the local population turned against the Jesuits, killing all eight of them. By then, the fate of Jesuit missionization efforts in North America had been sealed. In 1571, months before the violence at Jacán, Francisco Borja informed Menéndez that he was withdrawing the Jesuits from Florida because the conversion efforts had been a failure. At least one disgruntled Florida Jesuit agreed. Before departing for Mexico, Jesuit missionary Antonio Sedeño described the region as "the most miserable land ever discovered by man."

Following the Jesuit departure, missionary efforts in Florida stalled. It was not until the late 1580s that the Franciscans established their first permanent mission. Founded in 1587, the *Nombre de Dios* mission was the first of dozens of long-forgotten Franciscan missions established in Spanish Florida. Before the 16th century drew to a close, Florida's Franciscans had erected eight more missions, reaching north from St. Augustine to Guale (present-day St. Catherines Island, Georgia).

The early evangelization efforts met with mixed results. In 1597, Guale and Salchiche Indians in present-day Georgia killed five Franciscan friars. The so-called Guale Uprising left the Florida missions in ruins and raised questions about the entire missionary effort. By 1602, only three missions remained in all of Spanish Florida, with just five friars to serve them; but they were a dedicated few.

In 1612, in collaboration with one or more anonymous Timucua Indians, friar Francisco Pareja published a book of catechism and prayers in the Timucua language. And the following year, Pareja co-authored a Timucua-language confessionary. In 2019, Flagler College Professor Timothy Johnson uncovered one of Pareja's hitherto unknown Spanish–Timucua texts, a book of catechisms published in Mexico in 1628. Collectively, Pareja's volumes are the oldest published indigenous language texts from any region of the present-day United States. Pareja's work was created to assist the evangelization efforts of his fellow Franciscans, helping them to communicate the mysteries of the faith in the Timucua language, and warning them of the signs of idolatrous practices.

From the very beginning of their missionary efforts, friars also recognized the limitations of their authority over mission Indians. Peaceful mission life required negotiation and accommodation. In their efforts to convert mission Indians to Catholicism, friars tended to focus on specific native practices, such as polygamy and polytheism. Results were mixed. In the Province of Apalachee, for example, friars were never able to abolish the Apalachee ball game, a practice they regularly condemned as idolatrous. Native Americans throughout North America continued to deposit sumptuous grave goods with deceased relatives, a practice many friars simply ignored. Native symbols were often incorporated into mission architecture and design. Most friars recognized that alliances with indigenous political leaders were vital to their conversion efforts. When friars challenged local political authority or engaged in heavy-handed anti-idolatry campaigns, the response was swift and, on occasion, violent. During the 1680 Pueblo Revolt, for example, scores of missionaries and settlers were killed.

The result of the Franciscans' approach to missionization was that many indigenous traditions persisted throughout the colonial era. Native American political and spiritual leaders continued to exercise significant independence and autonomy, despite Spanish opposition. As anthropologist Robbie Ethridge noted, daily life for many mission Indians transformed into "a curious blend of old and new."

For the hundreds of friars who led missionization efforts from Florida to California, conversion efforts met with mixed results. At times, friars and mission Indians joined forces to resist pressures from royal officials or neighboring settlers eager to access native labor. Spanish archives are filled with joint petitions from friars and indigenous leaders challenging secular authorities or invasive settlers.

For Native Americans who constructed the missions, provided labor, tended livestock and assisted in military defense, the legacy was also mixed. Access to European luxury goods, livestock and metal tools altered the political and geographic landscape and, at times, enhanced chiefly authority over neighboring chiefdoms. At the same time, being part of the mission system came with its risks. With their congregated populations, mission settlements were vulnerable to regular outbreaks of disease. Between 1771 and 1820, death rates in the California missions exceeded birth rates, a pattern repeated in many other mission locations. Moreover, mission settlements were vulnerable to external attacks.

Beginning in the late 1650s, armed Indian slave raiders from the north began regular assaults on Florida's interior missions, with campaigns intensifying after the English founded Charleston in 1670. In 1704, Creek invaders from Carolina and their English allies launched a devastating campaign that destroyed the Apalachee missions. Thousands of Florida Natives were taken captive and sold into slavery in Carolina, while the missions were burned to the ground. Surviving Apalachee refugees fled east to St. Augustine or west to Pensacola and beyond. Thus, by the first decade of the 18th century, all of Florida's interior missions lay in ruins.

The decline of the Florida mission system preceded the rise of Franciscan missions in other parts of North America. In the early decades of the 18th century, the Spanish established 20 missions in Texas, the most famous of which was *San Antonio de Valero*, better known as The Alamo. In July 1769, friar Junípero Serra, O.F.M. (Order of Friars Minor), dedicated the first Spanish mission in Alta California, christened *San Diego de Alcalá*. By the time of Serra's death in 1784, nine more missions had been erected and, by 1823, 21 Franciscan missions stretched along a 700 mile stretch of coastal California, from San Diego to Sonoma.

Beginning in the late 18th century, the entire mission system came under increasing attack. Diseases such as smallpox had devastated mission populations and anti-clerical Enlightenment ideas increasingly challenged Franciscan aims. A growing number of settlers condemned the mission system for its perceived monopoly over labor, land and water. In 1833, the Mexican Congress passed the Mexican Secularization Act and, by the 1840s, all 21 California missions had been sold or seized.

Throughout North America, mission expansion accelerated Spain's colonial ambitions without requiring crippling financial investment in infrastructure and defense. Missions facilitated the flow of information and labor to colonial power centers; moreover, they helped to build critical alliances with distant chiefdoms, and they provided much-needed goods and supplies. Finally, the advancement of mission communities was often accompanied by another important frontier institution: the *presidio*, or military garrison. Together, missions and *presidios* paved the way for future settlements, part of Spain's long-term goal to expand its control over North America, challenging incursions from British, French and Russian competitors. However, building and maintaining imperial control over such a vast region was never an easy task. From the start of Spain's colonial efforts in North America, creating a reliable and efficient transportation system proved difficult.

Long before Europeans arrived in North America, Native Americans had forged a vast network of overland trails across the continent, a web of interconnected corridors for interregional trade and communication. These narrow foot trails often determined the specific routes followed by 16th-century conquistadors, and they played a central role in deciding the locations of early Spanish settlements and missions.

Over time, Spanish officials realigned some of these paths in an effort to reorganize the political and geographic landscape, a protracted process that unfolded over three centuries. Collectively, these various trails would come to be known as *El Camino Real*, or the King's Highway. Maintained by royal funds, the *Camino Real* was a network of disparate roads that stretched over much of the American south. Rather than a single transcontinental "highway," the *Camino* consisted of a series of pathways that connected missions and garrisons to more distant Spanish settlements.

In Florida, the *Camino Real* stretched west from St. Augustine to the Province of Apalachee and beyond, a distance of nearly 100 miles. Depending on the weather, the mode of transportation and the cargo, the journey could take anywhere between one week to a month. Yet, despite the challenges, maintaining a secure *camino* was critical to St. Augustine's survival. Shipments from Cuba or Mexico did not always reach the garrison town, and the city depended on the annual labor draft of indigenous laborers from Apalachee for trade goods, corn and other foodstuffs and, of course, information.

Coastal and inland waterways were also vital to Spain's colonial ambitions in North America. St. Augustine depended on regular shipments from the Spanish Caribbean and, at times, directly from Spain. Even the overland route into the Florida interior necessitated the crossing of the mile-wide St. Johns River, just west of St. Augustine, an obstacle that required a permanent labor force and a fleet of canoes. Coastal ports were also critical to Spain's colonization efforts. In the late 1630s, the Spanish established a port along the northern Gulf coast at San Marcos de Apalachee, just south of present-day Tallahassee, Florida. The San Marcos port opened a circum-peninsular maritime route to St. Augustine, as well as direct trade connections with Havana, Vera Cruz, Campeche and other Caribbean ports. Together, inland pathways and maritime ports were critical to the survival of the mission system and to Spain's imperial ambitions in North America.

Throughout its history, Spain's northern frontier was a complex and vibrant world, a multiethnic place inhabited by friars, soldiers, free Blacks, slaves, settlers and hundreds of different native peoples and polities. Over time, their interactions brought dramatic changes to Spanish North America, transforming the physical, cultural and geographic landscape — a fascinating, tangled tale too often overlooked in the history of the colonial United States.

REVOLUTIONARY WAR

Yo solo

Rayco Pulido

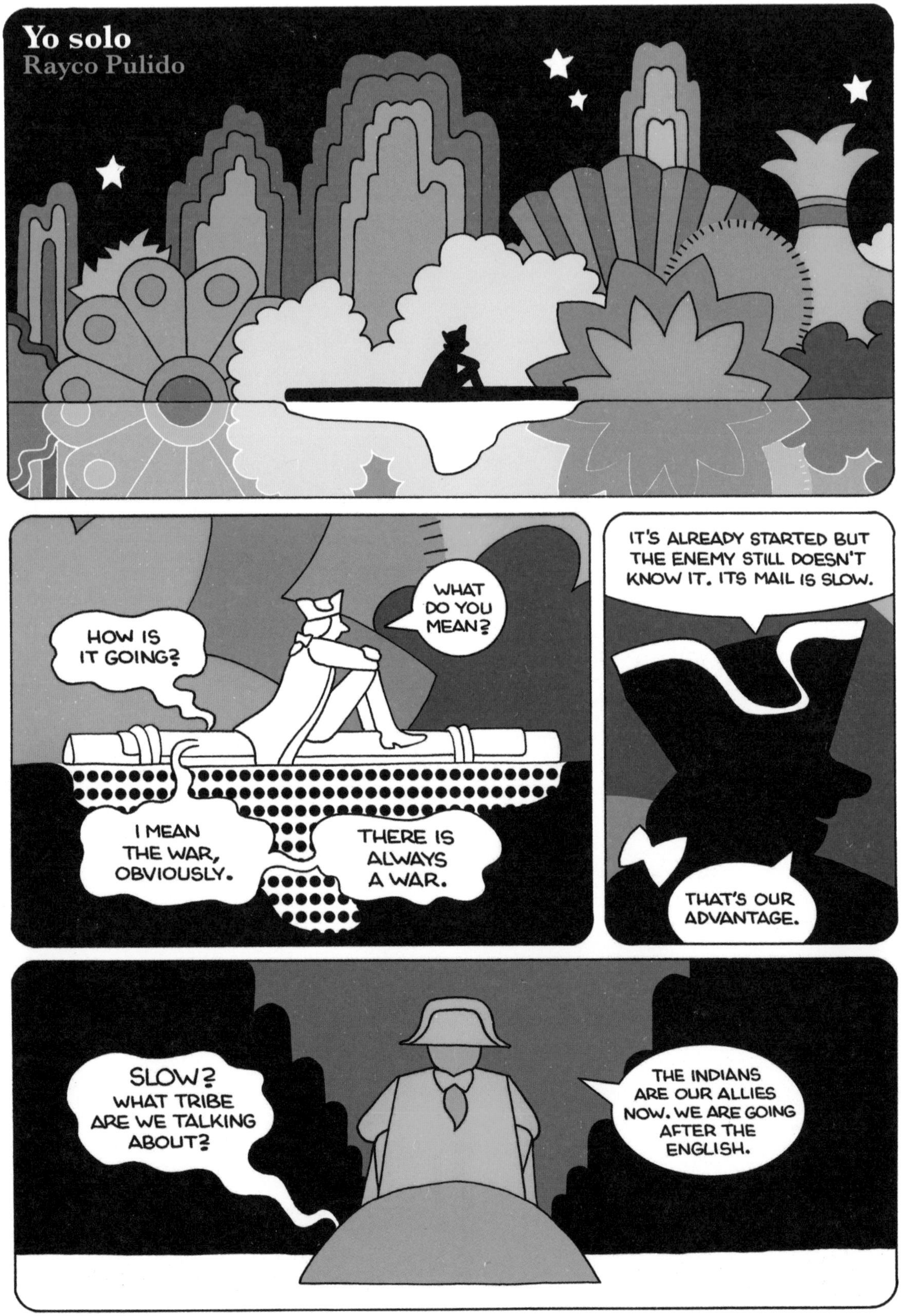

HOW IS IT GOING?
WHAT DO YOU MEAN?
I MEAN THE WAR, OBVIOUSLY.
THERE IS ALWAYS A WAR.
IT'S ALREADY STARTED BUT THE ENEMY STILL DOESN'T KNOW IT. ITS MAIL IS SLOW.
THAT'S OUR ADVANTAGE.
SLOW? WHAT TRIBE ARE WE TALKING ABOUT?
THE INDIANS ARE OUR ALLIES NOW. WE ARE GOING AFTER THE ENGLISH.

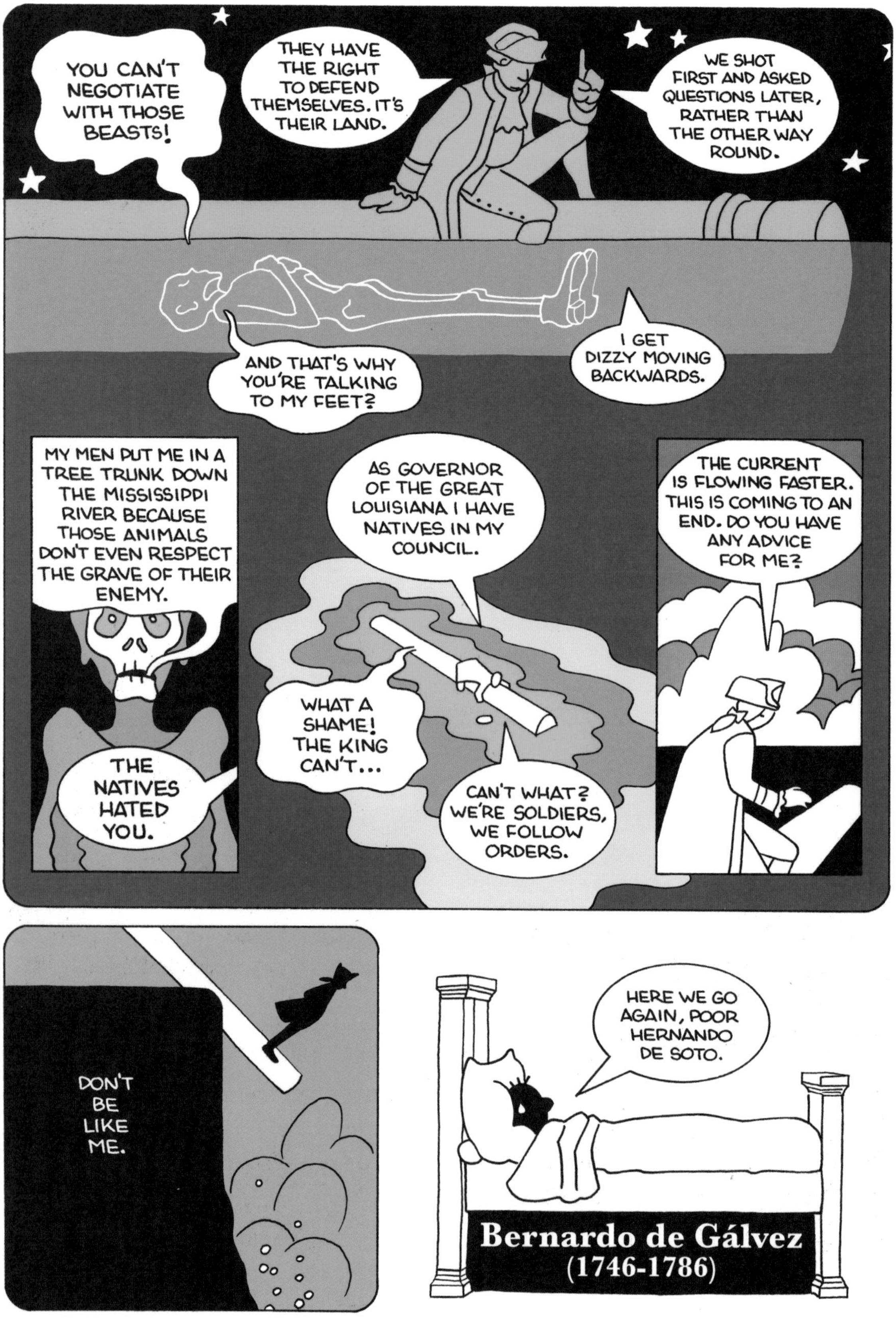
YOU CAN'T NEGOTIATE WITH THOSE BEASTS!
THEY HAVE THE RIGHT TO DEFEND THEMSELVES. IT'S THEIR LAND.
WE SHOT FIRST AND ASKED QUESTIONS LATER, RATHER THAN THE OTHER WAY ROUND.
AND THAT'S WHY YOU'RE TALKING TO MY FEET?
I GET DIZZY MOVING BACKWARDS.
MY MEN PUT ME IN A TREE TRUNK DOWN THE MISSISSIPPI RIVER BECAUSE THOSE ANIMALS DON'T EVEN RESPECT THE GRAVE OF THEIR ENEMY.
THE NATIVES HATED YOU.
AS GOVERNOR OF THE GREAT LOUISIANA I HAVE NATIVES IN MY COUNCIL.
WHAT A SHAME! THE KING CAN'T...
CAN'T WHAT? WE'RE SOLDIERS, WE FOLLOW ORDERS.
THE CURRENT IS FLOWING FASTER. THIS IS COMING TO AN END. DO YOU HAVE ANY ADVICE FOR ME?
DON'T BE LIKE ME.
HERE WE GO AGAIN, POOR HERNANDO DE SOTO.
Bernardo de Gálvez
(1746-1786)

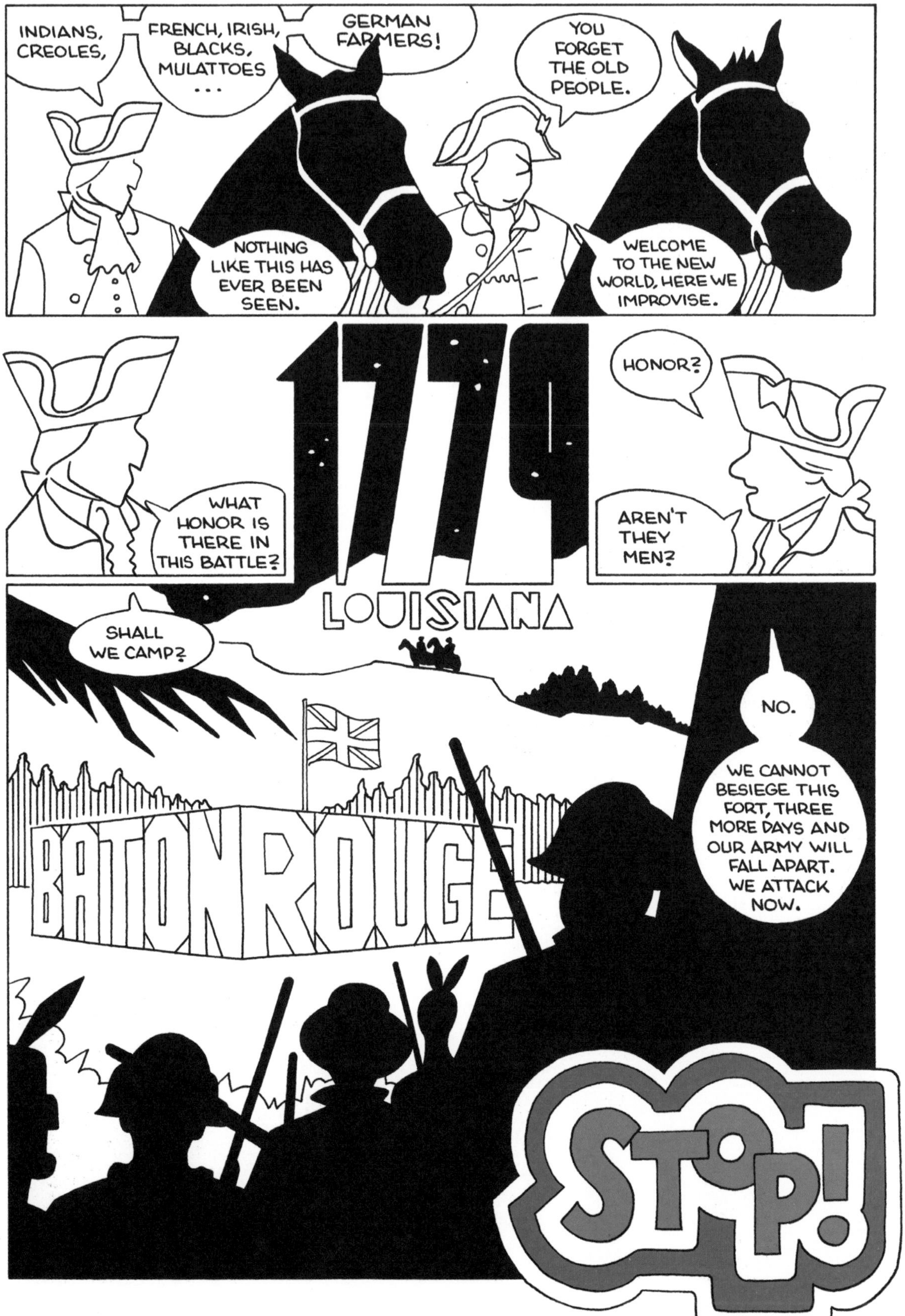
INDIANS, CREOLES,
FRENCH, IRISH, BLACKS, MULATTOES . . .
GERMAN FARMERS!
YOU FORGET THE OLD PEOPLE.
NOTHING LIKE THIS HAS EVER BEEN SEEN.
WELCOME TO THE NEW WORLD, HERE WE IMPROVISE.
1779
HONOR?
WHAT HONOR IS THERE IN THIS BATTLE?
AREN'T THEY MEN?
LOUISIANA
SHALL WE CAMP?
NO.
BATON ROUGE
WE CANNOT BESIEGE THIS FORT, THREE MORE DAYS AND OUR ARMY WILL FALL APART. WE ATTACK NOW.
STOP!

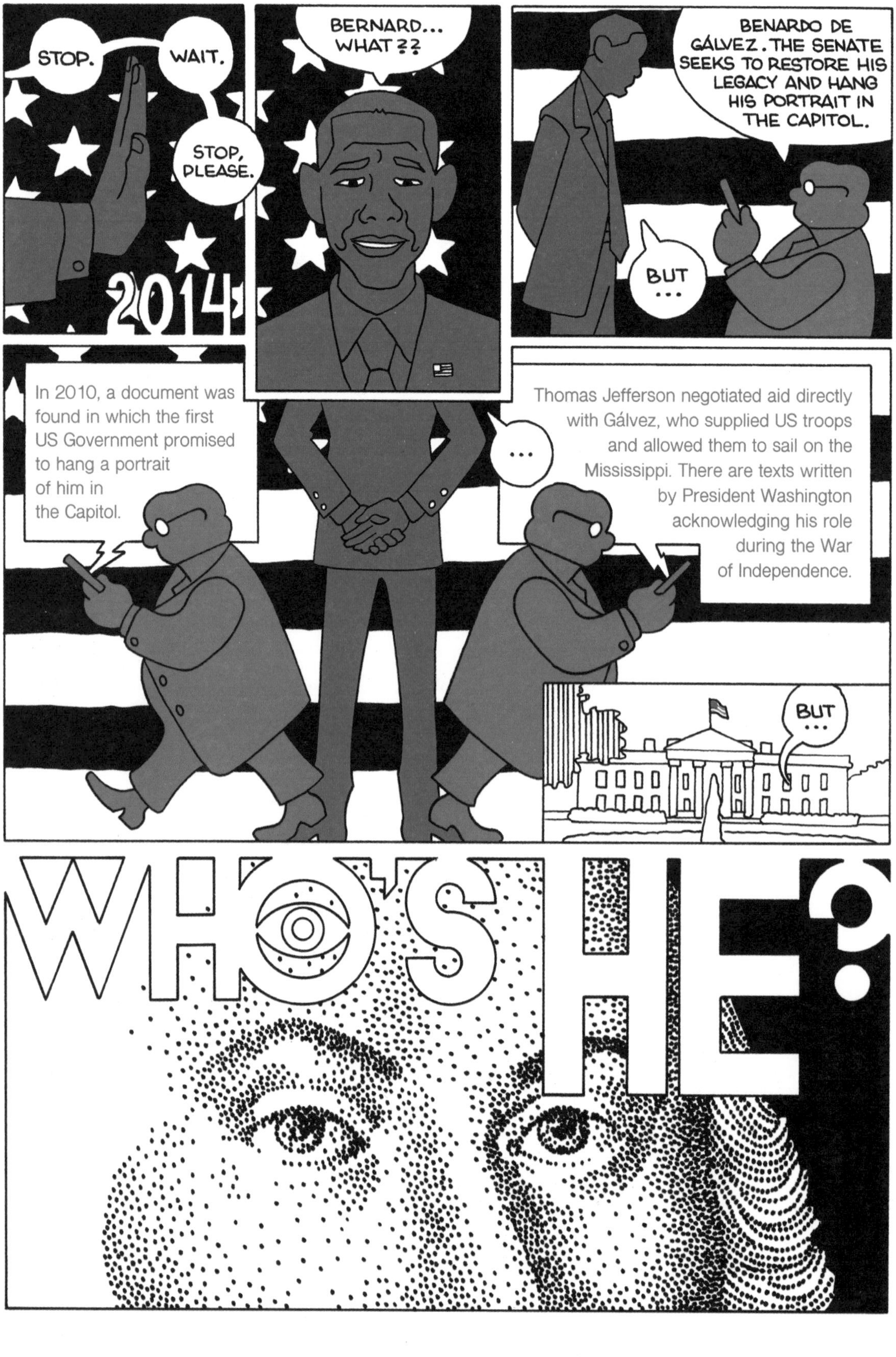
STOP.
WAIT.
STOP, PLEASE.
2014
BERNARD... WHAT??
BENARDO DE GÁLVEZ. THE SENATE SEEKS TO RESTORE HIS LEGACY AND HANG HIS PORTRAIT IN THE CAPITOL.
BUT ...
In 2010, a document was found in which the first US Government promised to hang a portrait of him in the Capitol.
...
Thomas Jefferson negotiated aid directly with Gálvez, who supplied US troops and allowed them to sail on the Mississippi. There are texts written by President Washington acknowledging his role during the War of Independence.
BUT ...
WHO'S HE?

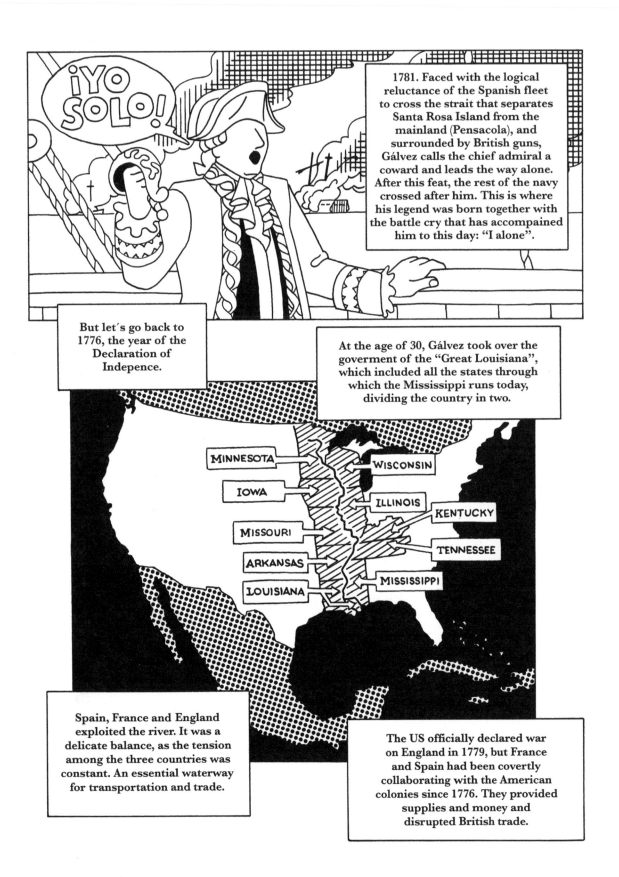

¡YO SOLO!

1781. Faced with the logical reluctance of the Spanish fleet to cross the strait that separates Santa Rosa Island from the mainland (Pensacola), and surrounded by British guns, Gálvez calls the chief admiral a coward and leads the way alone. After this feat, the rest of the navy crossed after him. This is where his legend was born together with the battle cry that has accompanied him to this day: "I alone".

But let's go back to 1776, the year of the Declaration of Indepence.

At the age of 30, Gálvez took over the goverment of the "Great Louisiana", which included all the states through which the Mississippi runs today, dividing the country in two.

MINNESOTA
WISCONSIN
IOWA
ILLINOIS
MISSOURI
KENTUCKY
ARKANSAS
TENNESSEE
LOUISIANA
MISSISSIPPI

Spain, France and England exploited the river. It was a delicate balance, as the tension among the three countries was constant. An essential waterway for transportation and trade.

The US officially declared war on England in 1779, but France and Spain had been covertly collaborating with the American colonies since 1776. They provided supplies and money and disrupted British trade.

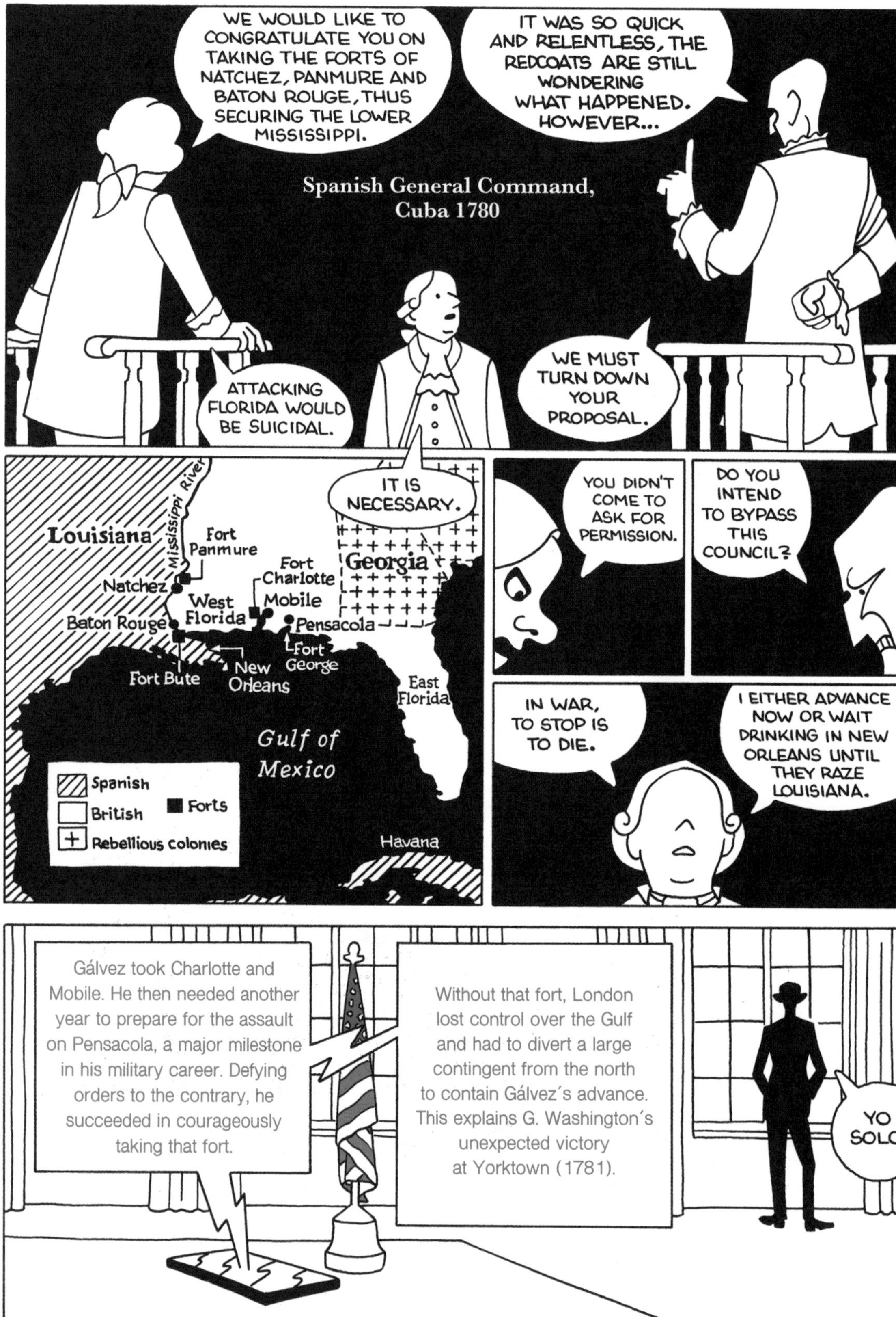
WE WOULD LIKE TO CONGRATULATE YOU ON TAKING THE FORTS OF NATCHEZ, PANMURE AND BATON ROUGE, THUS SECURING THE LOWER MISSISSIPPI.
IT WAS SO QUICK AND RELENTLESS, THE REDCOATS ARE STILL WONDERING WHAT HAPPENED. HOWEVER...
Spanish General Command, Cuba 1780
ATTACKING FLORIDA WOULD BE SUICIDAL.
WE MUST TURN DOWN YOUR PROPOSAL.
IT IS NECESSARY.
Louisiana
Mississippi River
Fort Panmure
Natchez
Baton Rouge
West Florida
Fort Charlotte
Mobile
Pensacola
Fort George
Georgia
Fort Bute
New Orleans
East Florida
Gulf of Mexico
Spanish
British
Forts
Rebellious colonies
Havana
YOU DIDN'T COME TO ASK FOR PERMISSION.
DO YOU INTEND TO BYPASS THIS COUNCIL?
IN WAR, TO STOP IS TO DIE.
I EITHER ADVANCE NOW OR WAIT DRINKING IN NEW ORLEANS UNTIL THEY RAZE LOUISIANA.
Gálvez took Charlotte and Mobile. He then needed another year to prepare for the assault on Pensacola, a major milestone in his military career. Defying orders to the contrary, he succeeded in courageously taking that fort.
Without that fort, London lost control over the Gulf and had to divert a large contingent from the north to contain Gálvez's advance. This explains G. Washington's unexpected victory at Yorktown (1781).
YO SOLO.

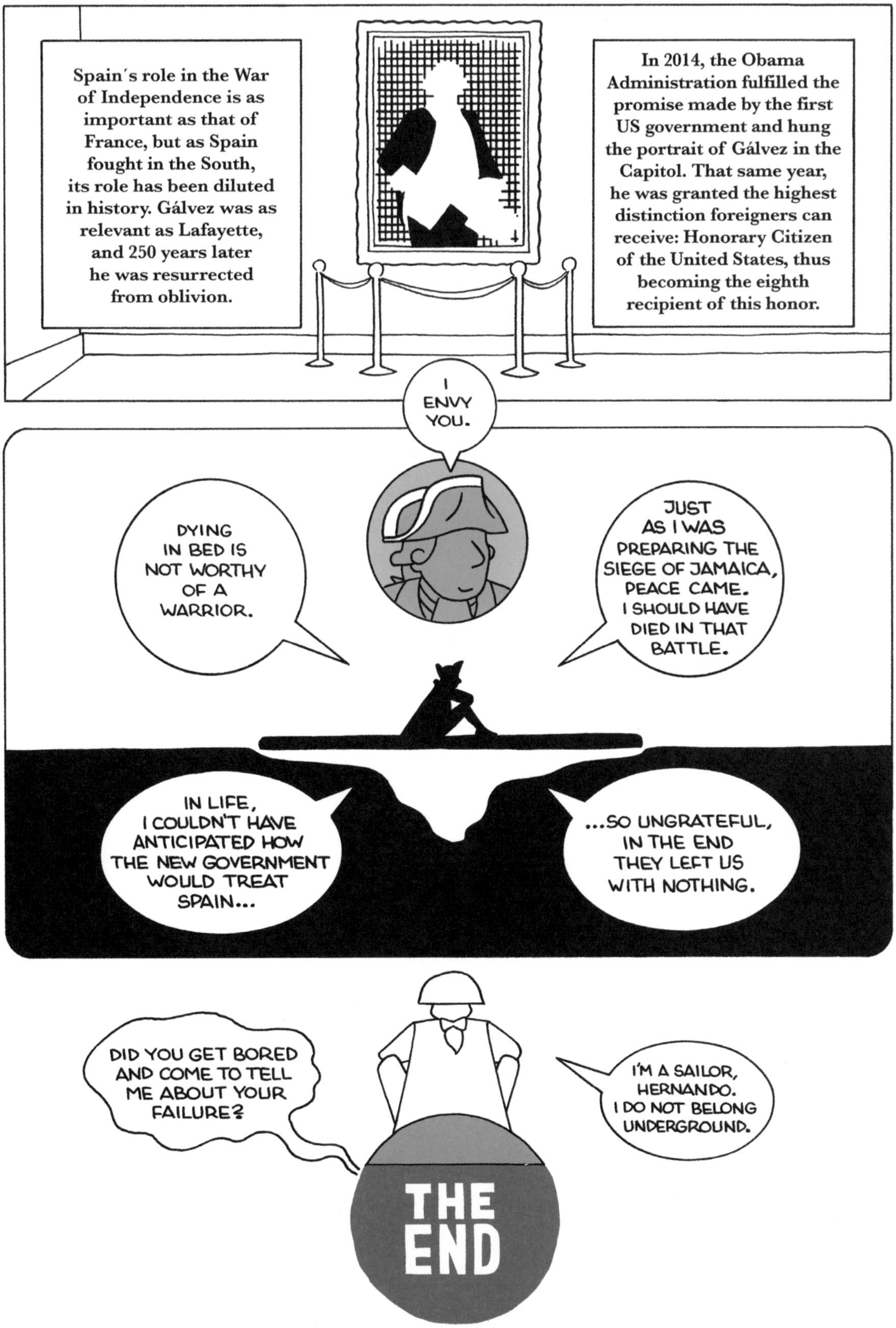
Spain's role in the War of Independence is as important as that of France, but as Spain fought in the South, its role has been diluted in history. Gálvez was as relevant as Lafayette, and 250 years later he was resurrected from oblivion.
In 2014, the Obama Administration fulfilled the promise made by the first US government and hung the portrait of Gálvez in the Capitol. That same year, he was granted the highest distinction foreigners can receive: Honorary Citizen of the United States, thus becoming the eighth recipient of this honor.
I ENVY YOU.
DYING IN BED IS NOT WORTHY OF A WARRIOR.
JUST AS I WAS PREPARING THE SIEGE OF JAMAICA, PEACE CAME. I SHOULD HAVE DIED IN THAT BATTLE.
IN LIFE, I COULDN'T HAVE ANTICIPATED HOW THE NEW GOVERNMENT WOULD TREAT SPAIN...
...SO UNGRATEFUL, IN THE END THEY LEFT US WITH NOTHING.
DID YOU GET BORED AND COME TO TELL ME ABOUT YOUR FAILURE?
I'M A SAILOR, HERNANDO. I DO NOT BELONG UNDERGROUND.
THE END

Bernardo de Gálvez

Eduardo Garrigues

DIPLOMAT AND AUTHOR

SINCE THE BEGINNING of the 18th century, England, France and Spain, the main European powers, continually warred against one another while trying to impose their hegemony on the world.

In 1754, these nations fought in what came to be known as the "Seven Years' War" in Europe and the "French and Indian War" on the American continent (with Spain entering the fray in 1761). Featuring an international array of combatants and fought in different theaters across several continents, this conflict is considered to be the first world war.

As a result of the British victory in said war, which ended in 1763, France had to cede much of its North American territory to England, including Canada; as compensation from the French Crown, Spain, which lost the territory known as Spanish Florida (west and east Florida), received the vast territory of Louisiana, including New Orleans at the mouth of the Mississippi River.

Little over a decade later, these nations were to clash again, in what became known as the American Revolutionary War (1775–1783), which ended in a victory for the fledgling United States and its allies.

An objective analysis of the positions occupied by the war's main combatants — England, France and Spain — leads us to believe that this conflict could easily have had a different outcome. At the time, it was difficult to envision that the American rebel colonies would succeed in establishing a Republic, which was unprecedented in the history of mankind; nor did it seem likely that a relatively small social group without a coherent political structure or an organized professional army would be able to achieve a military victory over the European power that had the most powerful fleet and army on Earth.

The leaders of the rebellion themselves — especially the Commander-in-Chief of the so-called "Continental Army," George Washington — understood that diplomatic, financial and military assistance from England's rival countries (mainly France and Spain) was essential in order to achieve victory.

Most of American historiography focuses mainly on the battles against England fought by the Continental Army, which was led by Washington and supported by France. However, the victory of the rebel colonies is owed in large part to the intervention of Bernardo de Gálvez who, from his position as the Spanish governor of Louisiana, managed to neutralize the British army's offensive on the Mississippi River and in Florida, thus preventing the British fleet from entering the Gulf of Mexico and the Bahamas Channel. Without this military (and financial) support sponsored by the Spanish Crown, Washington's army would have found itself caught in a pincer movement by the British army, which was attacking from several fronts.

Without exaggeration, we may characterize Gálvez's participation in that war as demonstrating exceptional conduct in an exceptional situation.

Regarding his social origin, it is enough to know that the Gálvez family came from the small coastal town of Macharaviaya in Málaga, and they did not belong to the high nobility; however, during the reign of the Bourbon dynasty, they held important political and administrative posts. Bernardo's meteoric rise through the military ranks and his appointment as governor of Louisiana came about partly thanks to the support of his uncle, José de Gálvez, who had been appointed Minister of the Indies under Charles III's reign and granted extensive powers over the vast Spanish overseas territories.

On the eve of the declaration of war against England, the young and courageous Málaga officer was appointed governor of a Spanish colonial territory neighboring England's possessions in North America. The extent to which his appointment was based on his own personal merits — as the young Gálvez had already proved his military mettle during the Spanish–Portuguese War, the Apache–Mexico Wars in northern Mexico and in the failed invasion of Algiers, where he was wounded — or due of the influence of his uncle, the Minister of the Indies, is irrelevant at this point. But the fact was that the territory of Louisiana would have great strategic importance in the war against England, which at that time seemed imminent.

Gálvez's success in this important new role was due in large part to his forward-thinking nature. This aspect of his personality is perhaps best explained by a brief sketch of his attitudes and actions before and after being appointed the Spanish governor of Louisiana:

- Before his post in Louisiana as Commander of the Internal Provinces of northern Mexico, Gálvez had already overcome the prejudices of the colonists of the time with respect to the natives, stating in his journals that the Apache Indians had their reasons for defending themselves from the white men who had invaded their territory.
- He ignored any racial stereotypes concerning the superiority of Europeans by valuing the contribution of mestizo, mulatto and soldiers of color in his troops and declaring that Black soldiers could be as brave and effective as their white counterparts.
- In his personal life, Gálvez disregarded the social prejudices of his time when he married Felicitas San Maxent, a beautiful Creole widow from New Orleans, which he did without waiting for the mandatory government authorization necessary to marry a foreigner.
- Gálvez anticipated Spain's declaration of war on England by enlisting and training the necessary troops to launch a military campaign on the banks of the Mississippi River and later to seize the strongholds of Mobile and Pensacola to take control of the Gulf of Mexico.

- After Gálvez's military successes in North America, when he was appointed Viceroy of New Spain, he recognized the equality between different social classes by frequenting dances, *cucañas* (greasy pole games) and other popular celebrations, something that none of the previous viceroys had done before.
- Among the positive aspects of Gálvez's personality, it is essential to mention his capacity to accept setbacks and to recover from failures due to factors beyond his control; for example, he faced adverse climatic conditions in the Mississippi campaign, in the occupation of Mobile and particularly in the siege of Pensacola, when a hurricane dispersed the ships of the Spanish fleet and caused many casualties among the troops.

While acknowledging the positive traits of Gálvez's vibrant and complex personality, we should also consider his character flaws. To objectively analyze this historical figure, we must paint a complete picture of Gálvez, warts and all.

Perhaps the best example of his complex character can be revealed in his feat of the siege of the fortress of Pensacola. On the one hand, Gálvez demonstrated great courage — bordering on recklessness — in this difficult situation; on the other, his proud and arrogant nature would cause a serious rift with the commander of the fleet that took part in that "amphibious" military operation (as the location of the British stronghold in Pensacola — at the bottom of a deep bay — required the support of naval forces to provide cover for the infantry troops upon disembarking).

To provide this support to the army, the ships of the Spanish navy had to enter the bay through a narrow channel, controlled by a British battery at the top of the Red Cliffs. Due to the difficult conditions for access and the threat of enemy artillery, the commander of the Spanish fleet, Captain José Calvo de Irazábal, defied the orders given by Bernardo de Gálvez, who had been appointed Field Marshal and, therefore, the Commander-in-Chief of the operation.

When Captain Irazábal refused to put his ships in danger of being sunk by enemy shells, Bernardo de Gálvez sent a dispatch challenging the sailor.

A 32 lb cannonball picked up in the encampment, which I lead and command, one of those being shot from the fort at the entrance. I bade those with honor and courage to follow me. I'll lead the way with the Gálveztown *to show you that you have nothing to fear.*

And when the commander of the fleet did not respond to this challenge, Bernardo de Gálvez decided to risk everything; aboard his small brig sloop *Gálveztown*, he managed to sail across the channel under the fire of the British artillery unharmed, and forced his entry into the bay, where the rest of the fleet would soon follow the example of their Commander-in-Chief. Shortly thereafter, the British stronghold would surrender.

When King Carlos III granted him the title of Count of Gálvez, his courageous act of sailing under the fire of the Red Cliffs artillery was immortalized in one of the quarters of his coat of arms, which was emblazoned with his ship and motto, "Yo solo" (I alone). It is best not to think about what could have happened if the enemy fire had sunk his brig, which may have meant not only the death of Gálvez but the failure of the whole operation.

However, in the face of this challenge, Bernardo de Gálvez acted as a modern-day businessman who jeopardizes the financial standing of his company by embarking on a high risk / high reward business venture. Gálvez believed that the King of Spain had entrusted him with the mission of neutralizing the British strongholds in the Gulf of Mexico, and he was willing to fulfill his duty at all costs.

As previously mentioned, history could have easily shaken out differently. If it weren't for Gálvez's military successes in the south and west theaters of war, the conflict would likely have lasted much longer, and the United States would not have gained its independence so quickly — or, perhaps, at all. However, history books do not always reflect the significance of Gálvez's military campaigns in Louisiana and western Florida to the war, which enabled Washington's troops and their French allies to win the final victory at Yorktown in the north (incidentally, to which the Spanish Crown contributed substantially by providing great financial support). The corresponding congressional resolution states that Bernardo de Gálvez was a hero of the American Revolution who risked his life for the freedom of the people of the United States and provided supplies, information and decisive military support to the war effort.

In 2014, Bernardo de Gálvez was declared an honorary citizen of the United States by the Congress — and, therefore, recognized as a Spanish and American hero; the same honor had been granted to the Marquis de Lafayette in 2002. The fact that the figure of Lafayette and France's contribution to the War of Independence in general are better known — and recognized — by the American public than Gálvez's efforts is due to both subjective and objective reasons.

Among those subjective reasons is the close friendship and collaboration between the French soldier, Lafayette, and George Washington, a relationship that could not be developed between Washington and Gálvez due to the great geographical distance between the northern theater of war and Louisiana. From an objective point of view, the determining factor was that, having lost all its possessions in North America in the previous war, France was able to declare war on England and recognize the rebel colonies without the danger of retaliation; Spain, on the other hand, had to anticipate and prepare for potential English attacks on its colonies in North America, which explains why the country took longer to declare war on England and recognize the US's independence.

Given his decisive contribution to the victory over England and the independence of a new country, Gálvez's achievement should take the place it deserves in the shared history of Spain and the United States.

IMMIGRATION

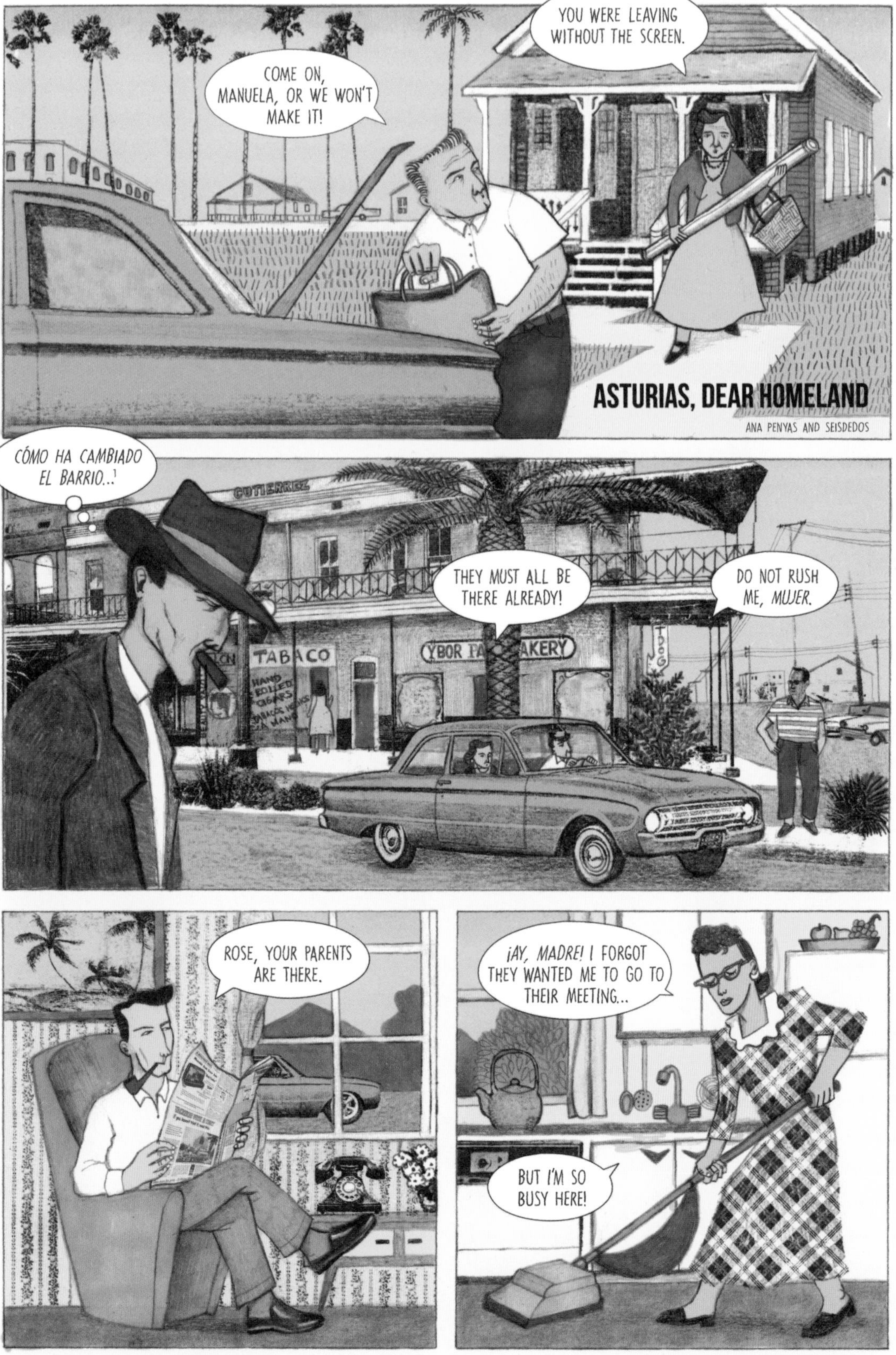
COME ON, MANUELA, OR WE WON'T MAKE IT!
YOU WERE LEAVING WITHOUT THE SCREEN.
ASTURIAS, DEAR HOMELAND
ANA PENYAS AND SEISDEDOS
CÓMO HA CAMBIADO EL BARRIO...[1]
THEY MUST ALL BE THERE ALREADY!
DO NOT RUSH ME, *MUJER*.
TABACO
YBOR
AKERY
ROSE, YOUR PARENTS ARE THERE.
¡AY, MADRE! I FORGOT THEY WANTED ME TO GO TO THEIR MEETING...
BUT I'M SO BUSY HERE!

1 GOSH, THE NEIGHBORHOOD HAS CHANGED SO MUCH...

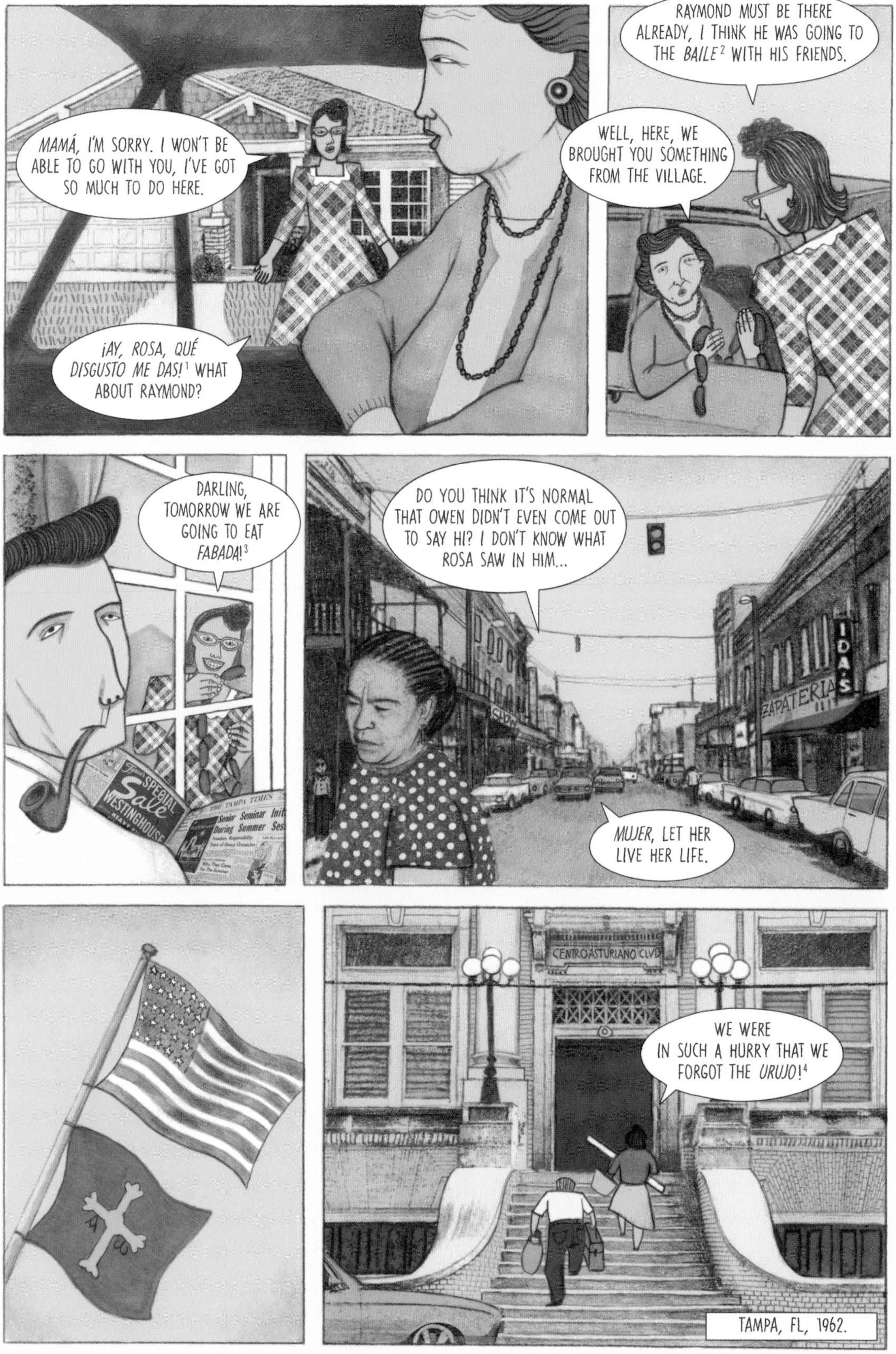
MAMÁ, I'M SORRY. I WON'T BE ABLE TO GO WITH YOU, I'VE GOT SO MUCH TO DO HERE.
¡AY, ROSA, QUÉ DISGUSTO ME DAS![1] WHAT ABOUT RAYMOND?
RAYMOND MUST BE THERE ALREADY, I THINK HE WAS GOING TO THE BAILE[2] WITH HIS FRIENDS.
WELL, HERE, WE BROUGHT YOU SOMETHING FROM THE VILLAGE.
DARLING, TOMORROW WE ARE GOING TO EAT FABADA![3]
SPECIAL Sale WESTINGHOUSE
THE TAMPA TIMES
DO YOU THINK IT'S NORMAL THAT OWEN DIDN'T EVEN COME OUT TO SAY HI? I DON'T KNOW WHAT ROSA SAW IN HIM...
IDA'S
ZAPATERIA
MUJER, LET HER LIVE HER LIFE.
CENTRO ASTURIANO CLUB
WE WERE IN SUCH A HURRY THAT WE FORGOT THE URUJO![4]
TAMPA, FL, 1962.

1 OH, ROSA, YOU BRING ME SUCH SORROW! 2 DANCE PARTY 3 A SIGNATURE DISH OF THE SPANISH REGION OF ASTURIAS 4 POMACE BRANDY FROM NORTHERN SPAIN

CENTRO ASTURIANO
TODAY
5 PM–ROCK & ROLL PARTY
8 PM–PASODOBLE
LEAVE THE KIDS ALONE!
LOOK, THERE IS OUR RAYMOND. SHALL WE GO SAY HI?
ACT NORMAL, GUYS, THE *ENCARGADO*[1] HAS ARRIVED!
DAMN *TABAQUEROS*[2] ALWAYS PLOTTING SOMETHING!
I WON'T VOTE FOR KENNEDY AGAIN...
REGARDS FROM THE HOMELAND!
I ALSO MADE *TORTILLA*.[3]
MANUELA, YOU'RE GONNA MAKE ME CRY!
MAESTRO, A COKE AND A BOTTLE OF WINE!
¡YO CREÍA QUE OS ÍBAIS A QUEDAR POR ALLÍ CURIANDO GANAO![4]

1 FACTORY FOREMAN 2 CIGAR MAKERS 3 A SPANISH POTATO OMELETTE 4 *I THOUGHT YOU WERE STILL OUT THERE, WATCHING THE COWS GRAZE!*

BUENO, PAREJA,[1] HOW DID THAT PENSIONERS' TRIP TO SPAIN GO?

YES! TELL US, HOW DID IT GO?

I'LL GO IN TWO YEARS, WHEN I RETIRE FROM THE FACTORY.

FIRST WE WENT TO MADRID AND LEFT OUR GRANDSON RAYMOND THERE FOR HIS SPANISH COURSE...

IT WAS...FINE.

CITIES SEEM A BIT MORE MODERN NOW, BUT THEN YOU ARRIVE AT THE VILLAGE AND NOT MUCH HAS CHANGED... ALTHOUGH MAYBE TOO MUCH FOR MY LIKING.

THERE ARE STILL FLIES EVERYWHERE!

IT MADE ME SAD TO SEE HOW LITTLE FREEDOM WOMEN HAVE...

...THEY SERVE THE FOOD AND THEN THEY DON'T EVEN SIT DOWN AT THE TABLE.

SO, THEY STILL KNOW WHERE THEIR PLACE IS!

¡AH, MUY BIEN! SINCE YOU WANT WOMEN TO BE YOUR SLAVES, YOU MUST LOVE FRANCO.

OK, OK. TENGAMOS LA FIESTA EN PAZ.[2] WE'LL SHOW YOU THE MOVIE OF OUR TRIP.

1 OK, YOU TWO   2 LET'S PARTY IN PEACE.

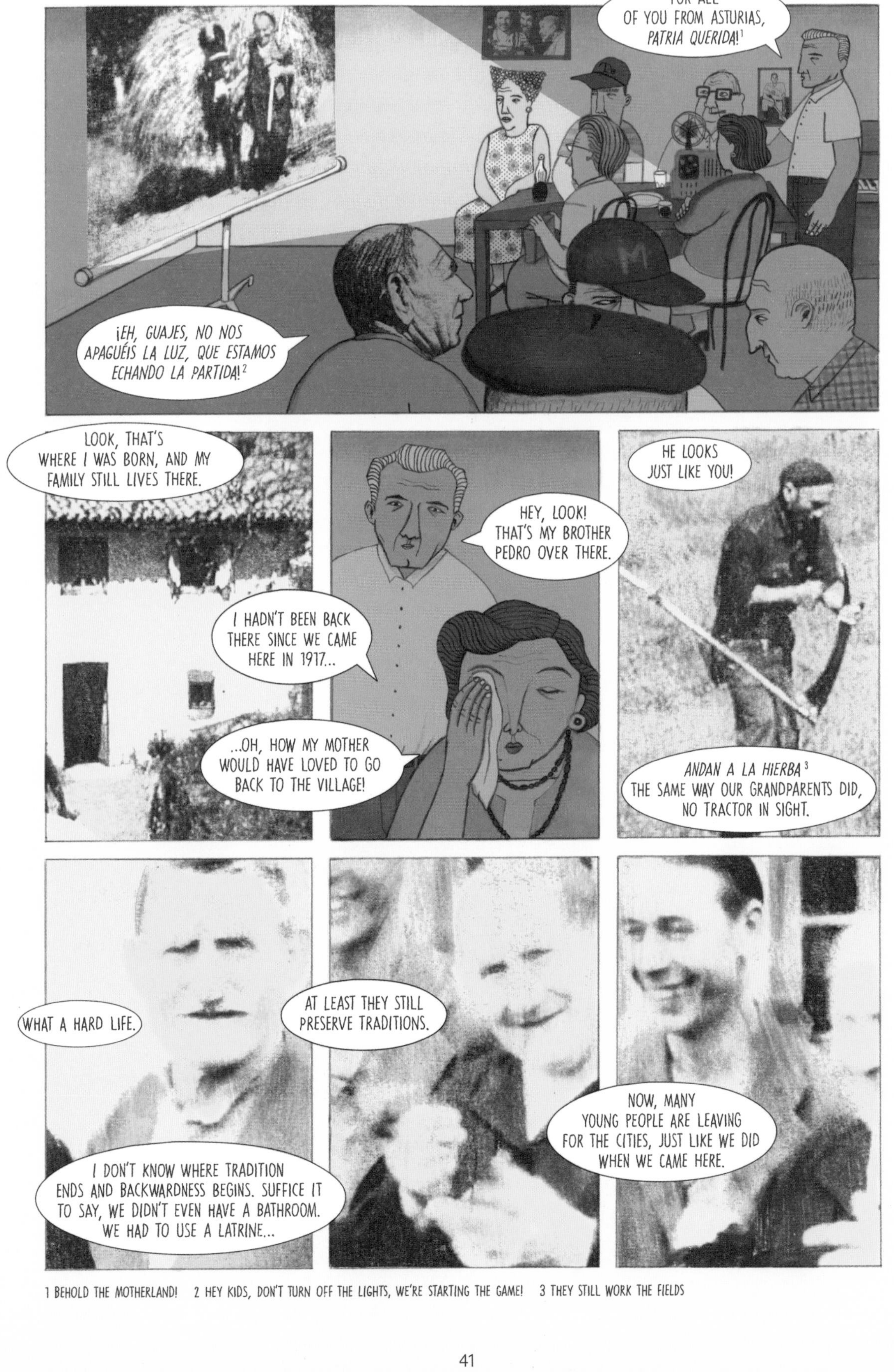
FOR ALL OF YOU FROM ASTURIAS, *PATRIA QUERIDA*![1]
¡EH, GUAJES, NO NOS APAGUÉIS LA LUZ, QUE ESTAMOS ECHANDO LA PARTIDA![2]
LOOK, THAT'S WHERE I WAS BORN, AND MY FAMILY STILL LIVES THERE.
HEY, LOOK! THAT'S MY BROTHER PEDRO OVER THERE.
I HADN'T BEEN BACK THERE SINCE WE CAME HERE IN 1917...
...OH, HOW MY MOTHER WOULD HAVE LOVED TO GO BACK TO THE VILLAGE!
HE LOOKS JUST LIKE YOU!
ANDAN A LA HIERBA[3] THE SAME WAY OUR GRANDPARENTS DID, NO TRACTOR IN SIGHT.
WHAT A HARD LIFE.
I DON'T KNOW WHERE TRADITION ENDS AND BACKWARDNESS BEGINS. SUFFICE IT TO SAY, WE DIDN'T EVEN HAVE A BATHROOM. WE HAD TO USE A LATRINE...
AT LEAST THEY STILL PRESERVE TRADITIONS.
NOW, MANY YOUNG PEOPLE ARE LEAVING FOR THE CITIES, JUST LIKE WE DID WHEN WE CAME HERE.

1 BEHOLD THE MOTHERLAND! 2 HEY KIDS, DON'T TURN OFF THE LIGHTS, WE'RE STARTING THE GAME! 3 THEY STILL WORK THE FIELDS

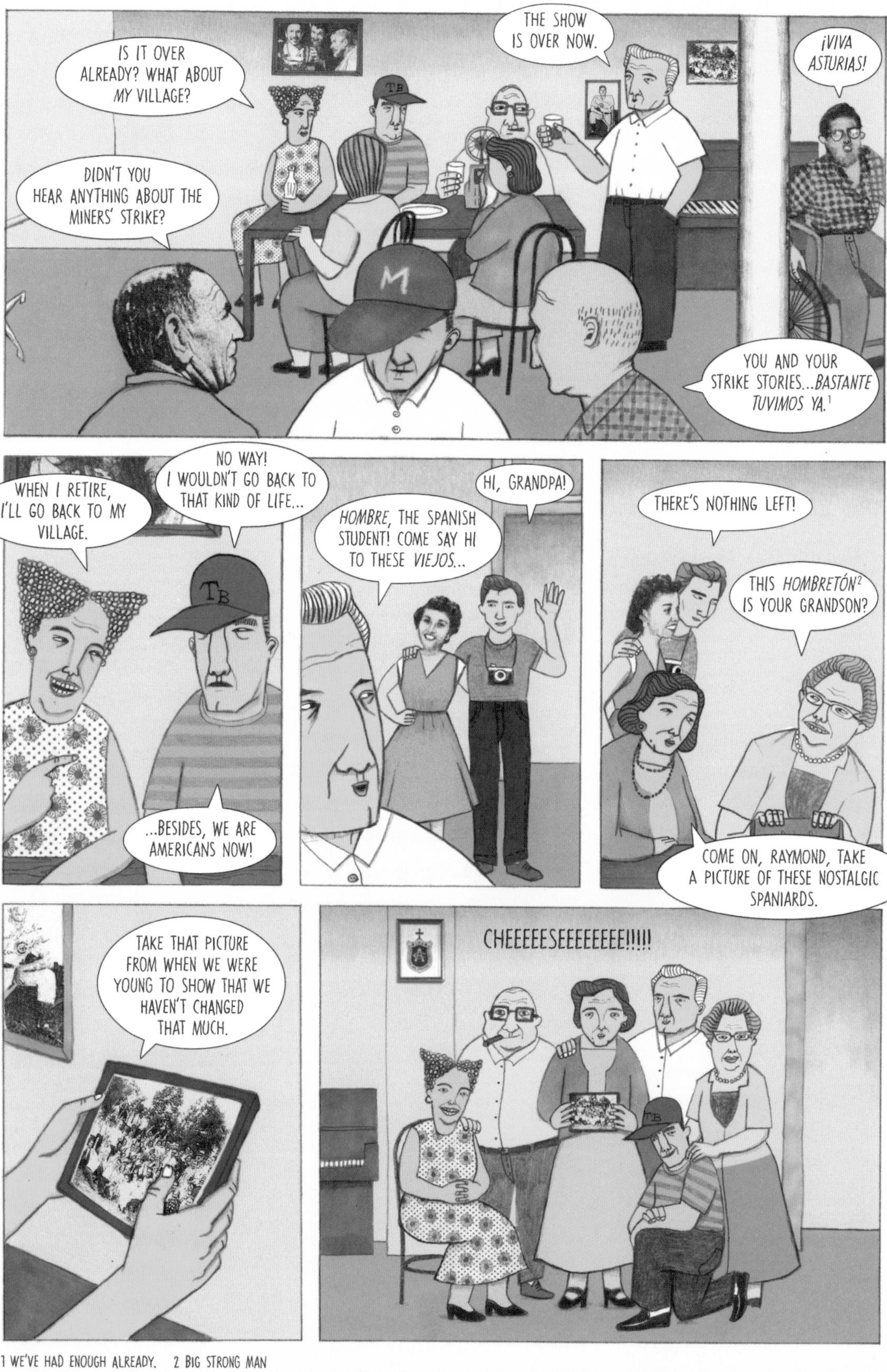
IS IT OVER ALREADY? WHAT ABOUT *MY* VILLAGE?
THE SHOW IS OVER NOW.
¡VIVA ASTURIAS!
DIDN'T YOU HEAR ANYTHING ABOUT THE MINERS' STRIKE?
YOU AND YOUR STRIKE STORIES...*BASTANTE TUVIMOS YA.*[1]
WHEN I RETIRE, I'LL GO BACK TO MY VILLAGE.
NO WAY! I WOULDN'T GO BACK TO THAT KIND OF LIFE...
...BESIDES, WE ARE AMERICANS NOW!
HI, GRANDPA!
HOMBRE, THE SPANISH STUDENT! COME SAY HI TO THESE *VIEJOS*...
THERE'S NOTHING LEFT!
THIS *HOMBRETÓN*[2] IS YOUR GRANDSON?
COME ON, RAYMOND, TAKE A PICTURE OF THESE NOSTALGIC SPANIARDS.
TAKE THAT PICTURE FROM WHEN WE WERE YOUNG TO SHOW THAT WE HAVEN'T CHANGED THAT MUCH.
CHEEEEESEEEEEEEE!!!!!

1 WE'VE HAD ENOUGH ALREADY. 2 BIG STRONG MAN

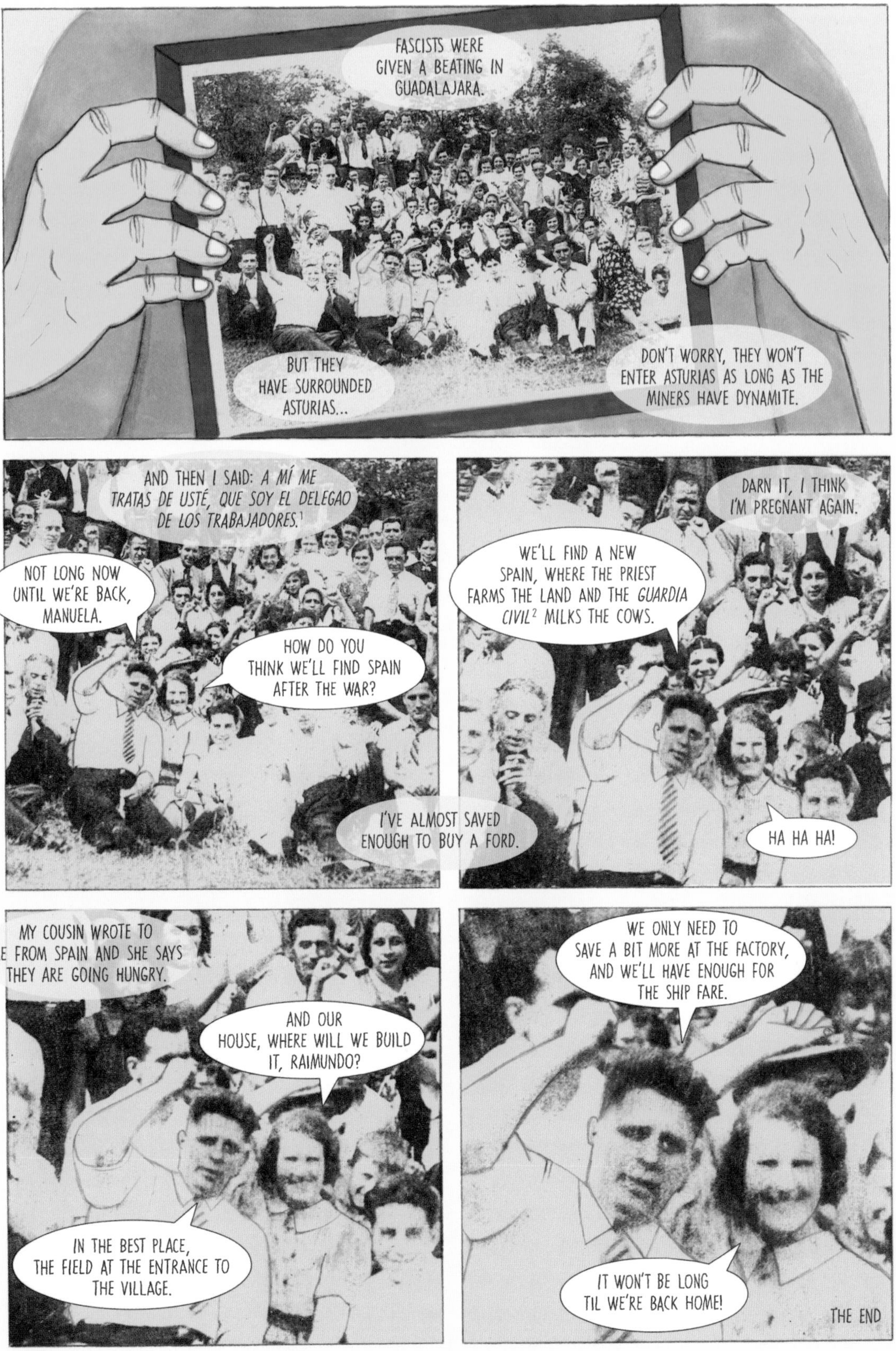
FASCISTS WERE GIVEN A BEATING IN GUADALAJARA.
BUT THEY HAVE SURROUNDED ASTURIAS...
DON'T WORRY, THEY WON'T ENTER ASTURIAS AS LONG AS THE MINERS HAVE DYNAMITE.
AND THEN I SAID: *A MÍ ME TRATAS DE USTÉ, QUE SOY EL DELEGAO DE LOS TRABAJADORES.*[1]
NOT LONG NOW UNTIL WE'RE BACK, MANUELA.
HOW DO YOU THINK WE'LL FIND SPAIN AFTER THE WAR?
I'VE ALMOST SAVED ENOUGH TO BUY A FORD.
DARN IT, I THINK I'M PREGNANT AGAIN.
WE'LL FIND A NEW SPAIN, WHERE THE PRIEST FARMS THE LAND AND THE *GUARDIA CIVIL*[2] MILKS THE COWS.
HA HA HA!
MY COUSIN WROTE TO ME FROM SPAIN AND SHE SAYS THEY ARE GOING HUNGRY.
AND OUR HOUSE, WHERE WILL WE BUILD IT, RAIMUNDO?
IN THE BEST PLACE, THE FIELD AT THE ENTRANCE TO THE VILLAGE.
WE ONLY NEED TO SAVE A BIT MORE AT THE FACTORY, AND WE'LL HAVE ENOUGH FOR THE SHIP FARE.
IT WON'T BE LONG TIL WE'RE BACK HOME!
THE END

1 TREAT ME WITH RESPECT, AS *I* AM THE WORKERS' DELEGATE. 2 POLICE AND MILITARY FORCE THAT PATROLS SPAIN'S RURAL AREAS

Ni Frailes Ni Conquistadores: Spanish Immigrants in the United States (1868–1945)

James Fernández

PROFESSOR OF SPANISH LITERATURE AND CULTURE, NEW YORK UNIVERSITY

Luis Argeo

JOURNALIST AND FILMMAKER

In the late 19th and early 20th centuries, the United States was home to tens of thousands of working-class Spanish emigrants seeking a brighter future.

1

With his crew on the brink of mutiny in the middle of the ocean, Christopher Columbus changed the course of history when he decided to follow a flock of terns that was heading southwest. That deviation would bring the Spanish expedition to landfall within a few days. If Columbus had not heeded those birds, the fate of the Spaniards would have been different. Some calculations suggest that the original course would have brought the caravels closer to the mainland: the Florida coast.

Four centuries later, thousands of Spanish emigrants would change the course of their lives crossing the ocean, this time with the Florida peninsula as their primary destination. They arrived in droves over five decades, and found their place in the tobacco industry — specifically, Cuban cigar manufacturing. Ybor City, founded in 1885 by a Spanish businessman who passed through Cuba, New York and Key West, and neighboring West Tampa, would be their new home. These emigrants did not seek glory, but rather opportunity, perhaps a lucky break. In Tampa, fortune would spread its wings again.

"It could have been Pensacola; it could have even been Mobile, in Alabama, or Galveston, in Texas. But fate wanted it to be Tampa." Rafael Martínez Ybor, born in 1929, knows very well the twists and turns that conditioned these emigrants' lives, as they are intimately linked to his own family history. His great-grandfather, Vicente Martínez Ybor, was one of the promoters of that tobacco adventure in Florida. Vicente's story takes us back to the shores of another sea, the Mediterranean.

Vicente Martínez Ybor (b. Valencia, Spain, 1818) arrived in the Caribbean as Columbus did, crossing the Atlantic with financial support. At the age of 14, he was fleeing obligatory military service. Family contacts connected this teenager to the tobacco business in Cuba. As young Ybor prospered on the island, he learned to live on the run. He fled his widowhood, he fled his own bankruptcy, he fled the War of Cuban Independence. He left Havana to save his fledgling empire from disaster, a tobacco emporium whose best-selling cigar was branded El Príncipe de Gales. In 1868, as Cuba's push for independence was heating up, he landed in Key West.

Another character must now enter this twisted tale: Eduardo Manrara, businessman and friend of Ybor whose propensity for seasickness made him choose the road over the ocean for his routine trips between New York and Key West. In 1884, on his way to meet his friend Ybor, he stopped in a small village on Florida's gulf coast called Tampa. Unlike Columbus, Manrara was following not terns, but guava. This fruit, prized in New York pastry shops, could make some money, he thought. It turns out that there were no guava trees in Tampa, but the detour made Manrara more familiar with the territory. Hot humid weather, cheap real estate prices, a railroad under construction, a large port — in sum, a perfect place for relocating the Cuban cigar business. Spanish tobacco entrepreneurs also sought to solve the growing problems caused by their unionized workers. Just as Columbus dreaded mutinies on his ship, businessmen like Manrara were wary of labor strikes in 1885. Similarly, they were men looking for land and the solution lay right in front of them: they would build a city dedicated exclusively to tobacco; they would create a huge cigar family and they would be the fathers.

On October 5, 1885, the first brick of Ybor City was laid. On April 13, 1886, the first "Clear Havana" cigar manufactured in the new tobacco town was lit.

Within a year, the factory where it was rolled, Sánchez and Haya & Co., would produce 500,000 handmade cigars per month. Eventually, thousands of emigrants, men and women, would produce cigars in 200 factories, live in the company town and run other businesses that flourished around the enclave. Emigrants from Northern Spain fleeing from misery, injustice and military service arrived at a place where, besides the cigars, everything was yet to be made. By the 1920s, Tampa would become known as the Cigar Capital of the World.

For years, Spanish, Cuban and Italian workers lived together in Tampa. Their clubs and mutual aid societies — *El Centro Español, El Centro Asturiano, L'Unione Italiana, El Círculo Cubano* — structured their social calendars, programmed recreational activities, musical evenings, sports leagues. Some built palatial clubhouses, state-of-the-art hospitals, stately cemeteries. In the early 20th century, Tampa was a unique town in the entire southern US: life was mostly lived in Spanish and measured in cigars. In 1929, more than a million cigars per day were manufactured in Tampa. Then, the Great Depression suddenly brought everything to a standstill. The demand for cigars bottomed out and caused many factories to close. Cigarettes killed cigars; machines replaced workers. Once again, our immigrants would have to reinvent themselves.

Many Spanish emigrants in Tampa — like their compatriots spread out all over the US in similar, if smaller, enclaves — had long yearned to return home someday. But the Spanish Civil

War cut that dream short. Many of them mobilized in favor of democracy. Some even went back to Spain to fight against fascism. But the outcome of that war — a fascist dictatorship, and a country in ruins — made Spanish *tampeños* (Tampans) realize that their lives, and the lives of their children, called for new dreams, new horizons. They were here to stay for good.

The majestic red-brick Centro Español in Tampa's neighborhood known as Ybor City is still standing, but it is now the centerpiece of a mall. Today, in front of that shopping center, Rafael Martínez Ybor contemplates a statue of his dapper great-grandfather, and wonders what memory will remain among the residents of Tampa — and of so many other places that were once home to vibrant Spanish immigrant communities — of the women and men who quietly, almost invisibly, sought decency and dignity, and, in so doing, helped build two countries.

2

If public monuments commemorating the presence of Spaniards in the Americas were proportionally representative of demographics, there would be far more statues of business owners — like Martínez Ybor — and miners or domestic workers than effigies of conquerors, explorers or friars. The phrase "Spain in the Americas" intuitively brings to mind the more than three centuries of Spanish rule in that part of the world; the era of those explorers, conquistadors and missionary friars so often memorialized in myth and marble. But in fact, the presence of massive numbers of flesh-and-blood Spaniards in the Americas coincides not so much with the heyday of empire, but rather, as in the case of Tampa, with its protracted demise and aftermath. It wasn't until the second half of the 19th century — by then,

only Cuba and Puerto Rico were still Spanish territories — that millions of working class Spaniards began crossing the ocean in search of opportunities they could not find at home. Most of those peasants and industrial workers headed for destinations in Spanish-speaking parts of the hemisphere. But tens of thousands of them would also end up settling in compact enclaves scattered all across "El Norte," the new emerging empire to the north with an insatiable appetite for cheap labor. Due to a complex set of reasons, their stories have been mostly forgotten; their statues are few and far between, almost invisible, just as they've faded in the public memory.

There was one case of a formal recruitment of Spanish workers to the US organized on a large scale: between 1907 and 1913, the sugarcane planters of Hawaii mounted a campaign that would eventually attract some 8,000 Spaniards to colonize and work on the plantations of the archipelago in this newly annexed US territory in the Pacific. But, for the most part, Spanish emigration to the US was structured by the same kind of informal or semi-formal, labor-driven networks that were at work in emigration to Spanish America. This process would play out thusly: miners or metal workers from Asturias or León would learn of similar work with better wages in places like Morenci (Arizona), Spelter (West Virginia), Donora (Pennsylvania) or St. Louis (Missouri). They would find their way there. If things worked out, they would soon send word for their partners, relatives and neighbors to join them. If the enclave acquired a critical mass, an enterprising immigrant might leave the mine or foundry to open a small business — a grocery store, say — catering primarily to her or his compatriots. If that proved successful, another might establish a shoe repair store, a laundromat, or a boarding house. Add to the mix a social club that functions as a mutual aid society, and you have the basic ingredients of a Spanish immigrant colony. During the last decades of the 19th century and especially during the first two decades of the 20th, this basic pattern repeated itself over and over again, at different scales, all across the United States, from New York to Hawaii, from Idaho to Florida.

Stonecutters from Cantabria would hear of better-paying quarry work in New England; before long, there are enough *cántabros* (Cantabrians) cutting granite in Barre, Vermont, to found and maintain a Spanish Workers Club there. Shepherds from the Basque Country, Cantabria and Aragón would become aware of opportunities herding sheep in Arizona, California, Nevada, Idaho, or Nevada; restaurants, hardware stores, hotels and social clubs would soon follow. Sailors from Galicia or the Basque Country would jump ship in the New York area and form Spanish neighborhoods near the docks of Brooklyn, Manhattan, or Newark (New Jersey). If they were cooks on the ships they might find work at a restaurant, or eventually open an eatery of their own; if shoveling coal was their specialty, there were many fires to be stoked on land: in factories, power generating plants, apartment buildings. On weekends they would meet not on the factory floor, but at the soccer field — or on the dance floor of La Nacional, the handball court of the Centro Vasco, the smoky cantina of Casa Galicia.

These waves of immigration often overlapped and interacted in unexpected ways. By 1920, there was already a significant colony of mostly Asturian metalworkers in the Canton–Cleveland area of Ohio; they would soon be joined by several hundred Andalusian miners fleeing from the labor unrest of the Rio Tinto copper mines in Huelva. Only in Ohio might the daughter of an Asturian couple yearn to become a flamenco dancer, the son of

an Andalusian couple might long to become an accomplished *gaitero* (bagpiper)...

Of all the Spanish immigrant enclaves in the US, that of Tampa, Florida, is probably the most emblematic. New York may have been home to more Spanish immigrants than Tampa, but the size and diversity of the megalopolis on the Hudson diluted the Spanish presence there. Tampa, in contrast, was a one industry town, and Spaniards helped build both the industry and the town itself from the ground up. Most of them would roll stogies of course, but the *colonia* grew so large that many others would provide goods and services to the cigar workers and their families. Other enclaves may have had modest social clubs; only Tampa's Spanish immigrants could boast of monumental institutions — hospitals, clinics, clubhouses and cemeteries — similar in scale to those of Havana or Buenos Aires.

Once a bustling mecca for Spaniards, Tampa represents one of the biggest examples of the broader phenomenon of Spanish immigration to the US. Ironically, though, even there, where the Spanish presence literally reached monumental proportions, the memory of this history has been almost completely forgotten. It turns out that the glue that held all of these enclaves together was composed of two main ingredients: economic hardship and hopes of returning to Spain someday. When the Spanish Civil War (1936–1939) dashed these hopes, and when post-World War II prosperity reduced their need for ethnic solidarity, the enclaves burst like bubbles; assimilation became the order of the day, and the memory of this collective phenomenon was largely relegated to the precarious, private realm of family lore.

HISPANISM

CONCHA ZARDOYA WAS A SPANISH WRITER, POET AND PROFESSOR
WHO SPENT 30 YEARS IN THE USA TEACHING LITERATURE IN
SEVERAL UNIVERSITIES ACROSS THE COUNTRY.
IN 1955, SHE PUBLISHED 'EL DESTERRADO ENSUEÑO' (THE EXILED
DREAM), A COLLECTION OF POEMS BRIMMING WITH NOSTALGIA
AND VERSES DEDICATED TO SPAIN AND ITS WRITERS. THIS STORY
ILLUSTRATES THE POEM THAT OPENS THE COLLECTION,
'LOS DESTERRADOS' (THE EXILES), AND IT ALSO INCLUDES
IMAGES FROM OTHER TEXTS THAT MAKE UP THIS BOOK,
SUCH AS 'COMO UN ALTO NAVÍO, EL RASCACIELOS' (AS A HIGH
VESSEL, THE SKYSCRAPER), 'TRES MUJERES, SOMBRAS NEGRAS'
(THREE WOMEN, BLACK SHADOWS) OR '¡YA NADIE TE QUIERE,
VERDE!' (NO ONE LOVES YOU ANYMORE, GREEN!), AN ELEGY
DEDICATED TO FEDERICO GARCÍA LORCA.

THIS IS ALSO A TRIBUTE TO ALL THE SPANISH FEMALE WRITERS
FORGOTTEN BY HISTORY.

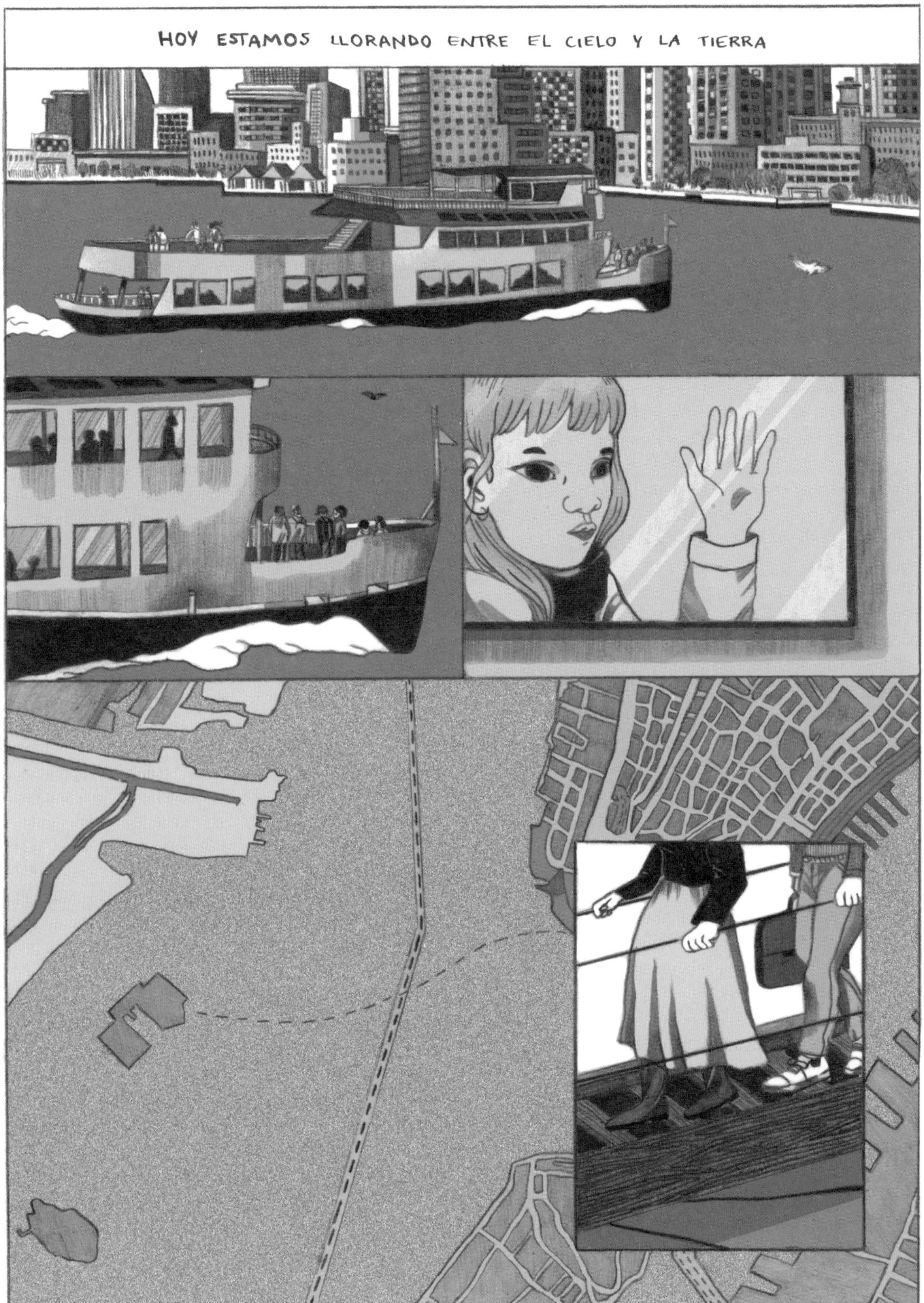
HOY ESTAMOS LLORANDO ENTRE EL CIELO Y LA TIERRA
¿HA CAÍDO LA LLUVIA, EL CRUEL SOL DE LOS TRÓPICOS,

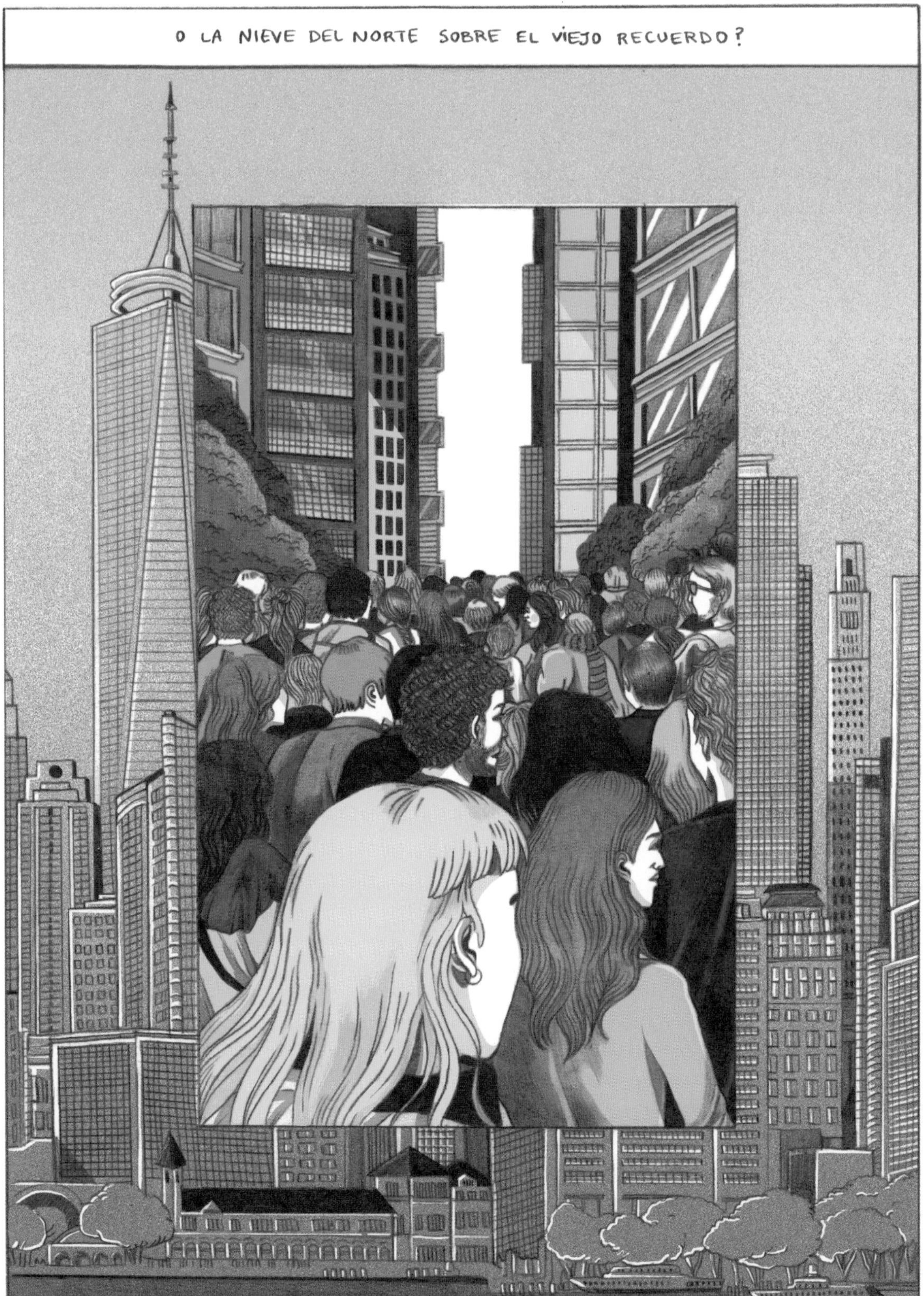
O LA NIEVE DEL NORTE SOBRE EL VIEJO RECUERDO?
EL AMOR ES ANTIGUO; NOS RODEA LOS OJOS LA PROFUNDA TRISTEZA

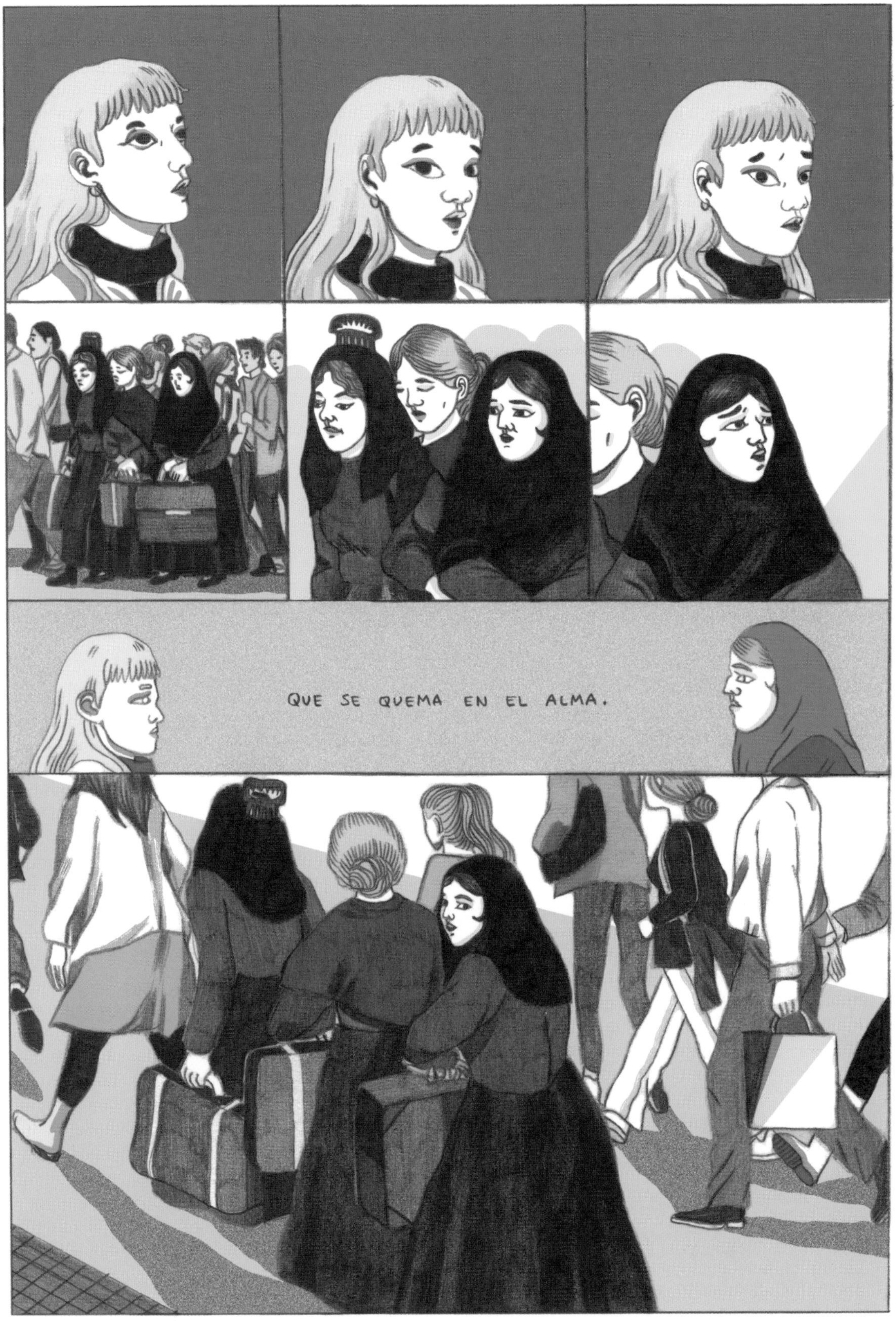
QUE SE QUEMA EN EL ALMA.

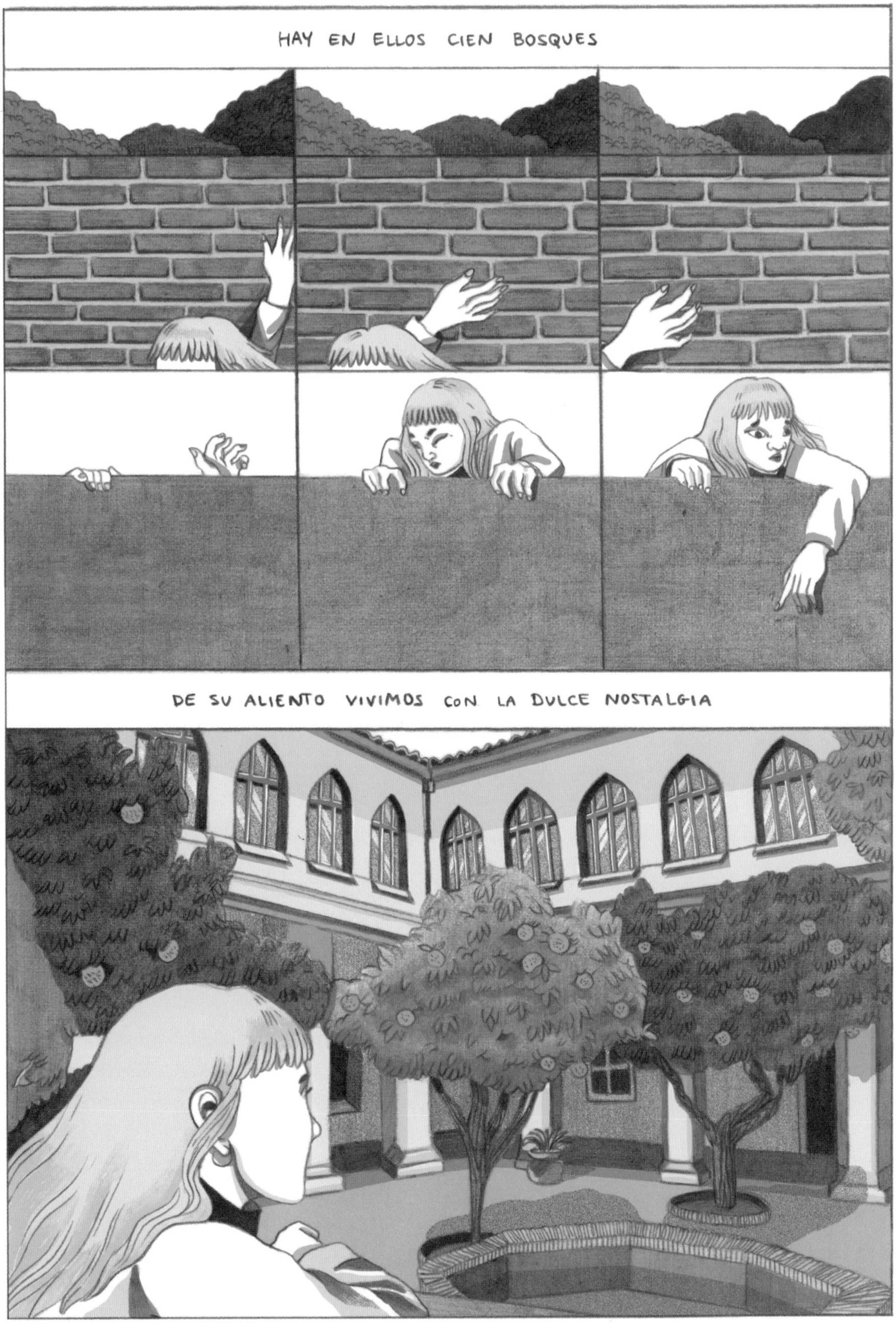
HAY EN ELLOS CIEN BOSQUES
DE SU ALIENTO VIVIMOS CON LA DULCE NOSTALGIA

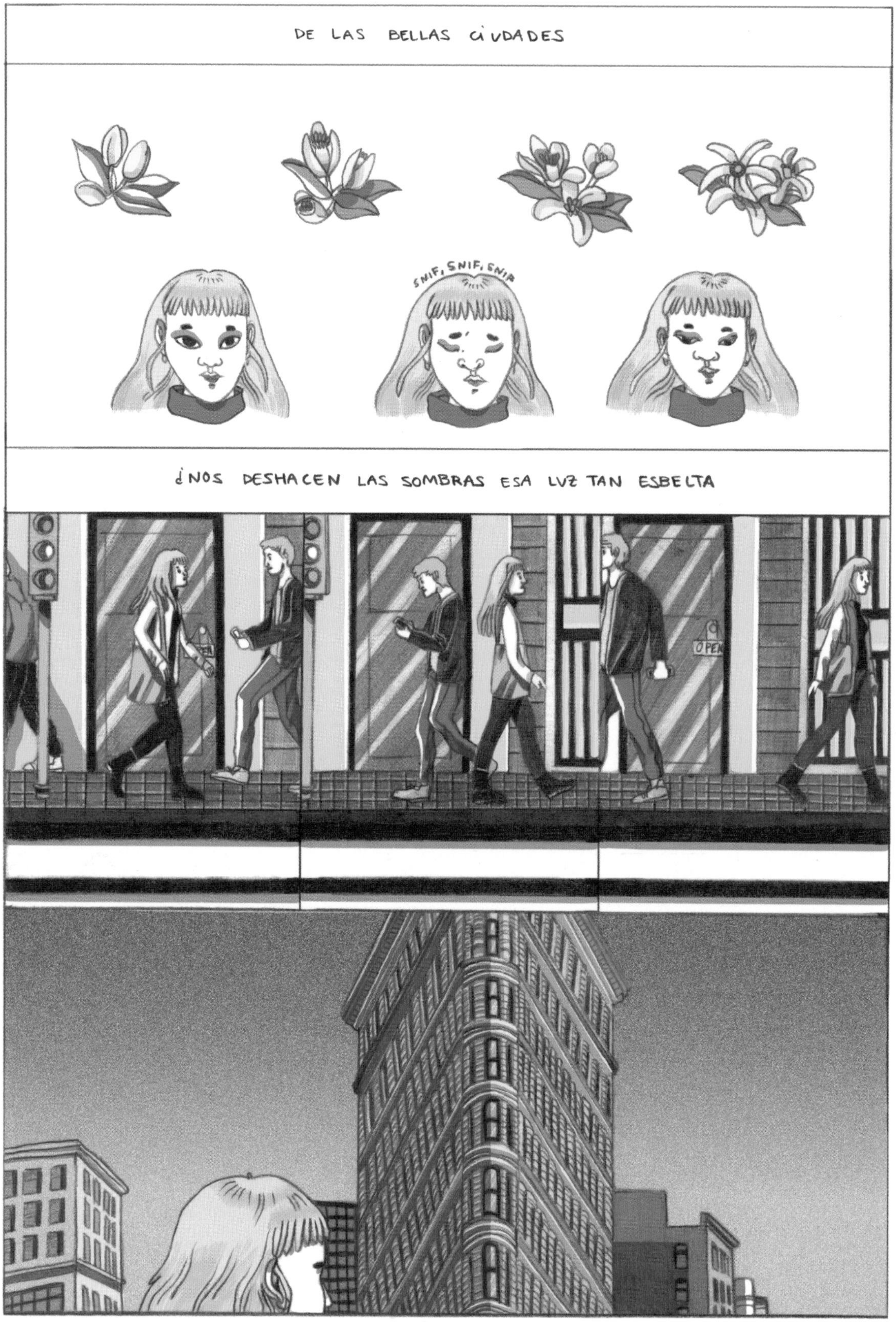
DE LAS BELLAS CIUDADES
SNIF, SNIF, SNIF
¿NOS DESHACEN LAS SOMBRAS ESA LUZ TAN ESBELTA
OPEN

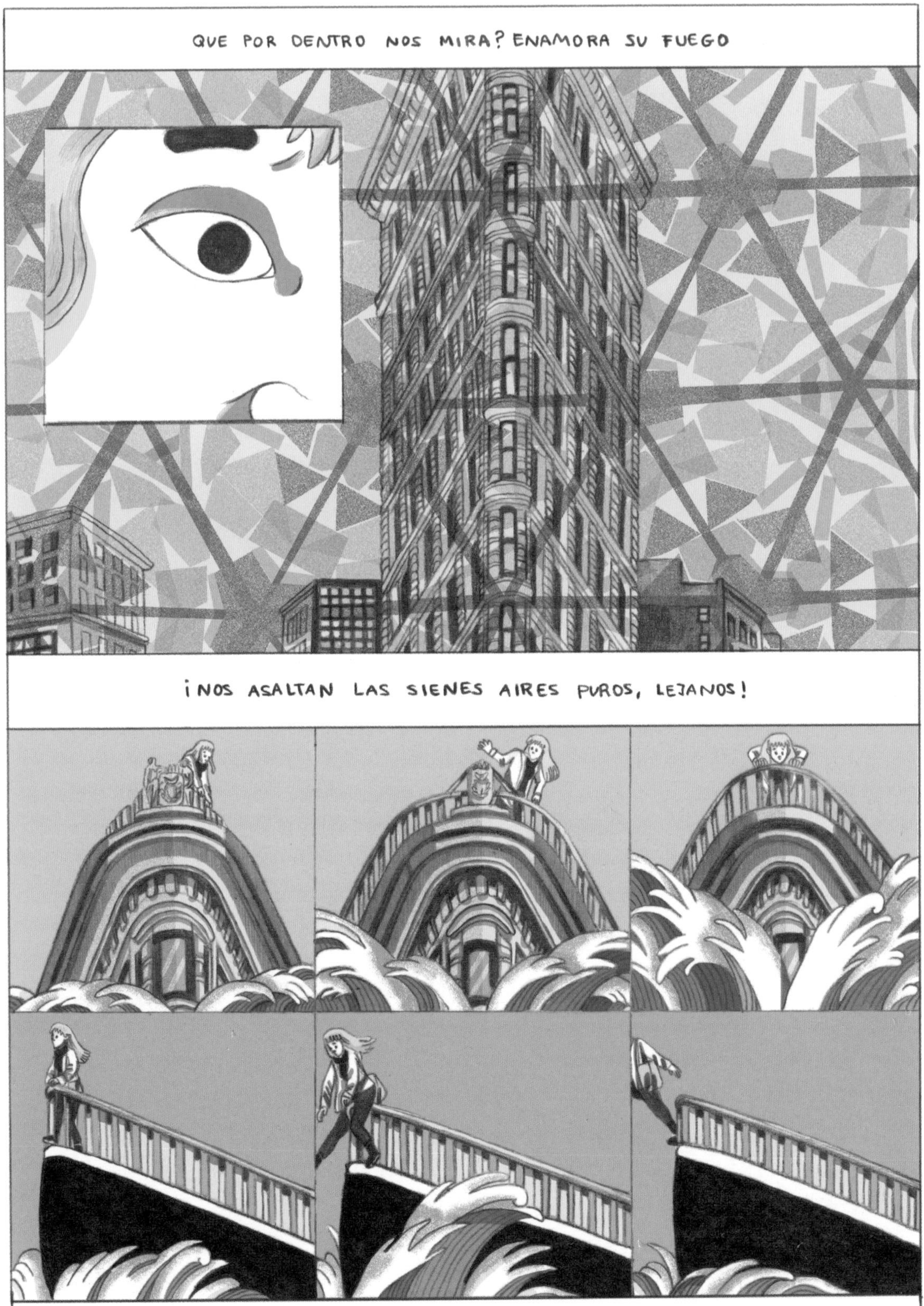
QUE POR DENTRO NOS MIRA? ENAMORA SU FUEGO
¡NOS ASALTAN LAS SIENES AIRES PUROS, LEJANOS!
¿VIENEN SIEMPRE DE ESPAÑA? ¿NO NOS MIENTE EL ANHELO?

¡AH, VOLVER A SER NIÑOS TIERNAMENTE QUEREMOS!

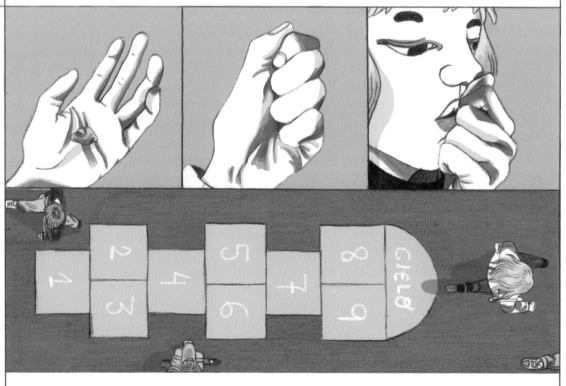

EN EL SUEÑO JUGAMOS Y OLVIDAMOS LA HISTORIA.

THE EXILES

WE ARE WEEPING TODAY
BETWEEN THE EARTH AND THE SKY.

HAS THE RAIN FALLEN,
THE CRUEL SUN OF THE TROPICS
OR THE SNOWS OF THE NORTH,
ONTO THAT OLD MEMORY?

LOVE IS ANCIENT:
THE PROFOUND SORROW
THAT BURNS IN ONE'S SOUL
ENCIRCLES THE EYES.

ONE HUNDRED FORESTS LAY WITHIN:
FROM THEIR BREATH WE LIVE
OFF THE SWEET YEARNING
OF GLAMOROUS CITIES.

THAT SLIM LIGHT
THAT PEERS INSIDE US,
DOES IT DISSOLVE THE SHADOWS?
ITS FIRE ENAMORS!

PURE, DISTANT AIR
STORMS OUR TEMPLES!
DO THEY ALWAYS COME FROM SPAIN?
MIGHT THE LONGING DECEIVE US?

AH, TO BE CHILDREN AGAIN,
WE TENDERLY WISH!
IN OUR DREAMS WE PLAY
AND FORGET ABOUT HISTORY.

FROM 'THE EXILED DREAM'
TRANSLATED BY ELIZABETH POLLI

The Spanish Philological and Literary Legacy in the United States

Lucía Cotarelo Esteban

POSTDOCTORAL RESEARCHER, AUTONOMOUS UNIVERSITY OF BARCELONA

AMERICA'S LOVE FOR all things Spanish was born at the end of the 18th century and spread throughout the 19th century, propelled by a romantic interest in spaces and cultures that were considered exotic. This idealized vision, which used to fall into the folkloric stereotype — Spain was once considered an "authentic" nation frozen in time — spread through the works, diaries and travel books of authors such as Prescott, Ticknor and Irving. The interest in Spanish culture extended to its language, which is why since the mid-19th century studies on Spanish culture and its language started becoming institutionalized and more professional. The US's motives for this interest soon shifted from pure romanticism to more utilitarian reasons related to their political and economic intentions with respect to the Spanish American colonies — with which the US wished to establish diplomatic and commercial ties — and in response to the outbreak of World War I (1914–1918). The war had two major effects on the relationship between the world powers of the United States and Spain. On the one hand, the presence of the German language in American classrooms went into decline and was replaced by Spanish, a language that was becoming more and more popular in the US, and more Spanish teachers were hired as a result. On the other, Spanish scholars and scientists began limiting their exchange programs and trips to European countries to avoid conflict and increased their travel to the United States.

At the same time, there was an increase not only in the number of Spanish courses being taught in universities throughout the country, but also in the number of translations of popular literary works of the time. New York became the epicenter of this translation boom, and it was there that the main Spanish-language newspaper was born, *La Prensa*. Established in 1913 as a weekly paper and published by José Camprubí as a daily since 1918, *La Prensa* contained Spanish novels in installments, as well as collections of short stories and poetry, profiles of Spanish intellectuals, news about their academic world and their stays in New York and news about Spain, its language and its dissemination in the United States.

Thus, a friendly cultural relationship between the United States and Spain was built on America's interest in Hispanism, which bore its greatest fruit in the first third of the 20th century and encouraged more and more Spanish intellectuals and artists to cross the Atlantic. The main driver of this emigration was the growing need for Spanish teachers: to meet this need, in the 1910s and 1920s, Hispanists Federico de Onís and Carolina Marcial Dorado, among others, joined Columbia University and Barnard College, respectively, and poet León Felipe joined the universities of Columbia and Cornell in New York. Other writers who also travelled to this city during this time created, through their works, an image of American cities and culture among Spanish people that was full of ambiguities: Juan Ramón Jiménez in his *Diary of a Newlywed Poet* (1916), José Moreno Villa in his *Crónicas de Pruebas de Nueva York* (*Observations of New York*, 1927), Teresa de Escoriaza in her novel *El Crisol de las Razas* (The Crucible of the Races, 1929), Julio Camba in *The Automatic City* (1934), or Federico García Lorca in his *Poet in New York* (1940).

Regarding Hispanist researchers and professors arriving in the US, it is important to understand the formal collaborative context in which these trips took place: that of cultural and university institutions. During the last decades of the 19th century and the first decades of the 20th century, cultural, scientific and research institutions were created in Spain, such as the *Institución Libre de Enseñanza* (Free Teaching Institution, 1876), the *Junta para Ampliación de Estudios* (Committee for the Promotion of Studies and Scientific Research, 1907), its *Residencia de Estudiantes* (Residential College, 1910) and its *Residencia de Señoritas* (Residential College for Women, 1915). In the United States, institutions dedicated to the dissemination of Hispanism were also created, such as the Hispanic Society (New York, 1904), created by Archer Milton Huntington, and the *Instituto de las Españas* at Columbia University (1920). These institutions came into contact with one another thanks to the work of a number of American intellectuals, including Alice Gulick, a professor at Mount Holyoke College, who founded the International Institute for Girls in Spain (1877) — later renamed the International Institute for Education — and Susan Huntington, who directed the Institute from 1910 to 1918. Gulick and Huntington were the first major promoters of these transatlantic collaborations between Spain and the US and maintained a close relationship with Spaniards such as María Goyri, Zenobia Camprubí and María de Maeztu who, along with many others such as José Castillejo — President of the aforementioned JAE — were committed to promoting exchanges between students and teachers from both countries. These were organized by the JAE, the *Instituto de las Españas* in New York — directed by Federico de Onis — and many American universities, including women's colleges such as Smith and Vassar. These exchanges were interrupted by the Spanish Civil War, but the International Institute took them up again in the 1940s, promoting the entry of Spanish students and scholars such as Julián Marías and Carlos Bousoño into US universities.

When the Spanish Civil War (1936–1939) broke out, the United States officially stood neutral; however, a group of volunteers who formed the Lincoln Brigade participated directly in the conflict in favor of the Spanish Second Republic. The American artistic and intellectual community started a support movement through unions, associations and magazines. Some of them, such as the *Art Front* and the *New Masses*, published excerpts of works by Spanish and American authors on the Spanish War. At the end of the conflict, the United States maintained rigid immigration quotas and denied asylum requests from Spaniards, prioritizing the entry of a considerable number of scholars offered positions by US institutions. In view of the growing demand for Spanish language courses, and thanks to the connections established during the previous decades, among those most favored by these measures were philologists and writers, as well as scholars specialized in various fields who were then "converted" into teaching Spanish or working in translation or dubbing. The Spanish language thus became the greatest intangible heritage of Spanish exiles in the United States, facilitating their access to jobs. Despite these circumstances, few of them arrived directly from Europe: most were forced to move to other Spanish-speaking countries, where they would live for months or even years before emigrating again to the US in search of better economic conditions.

Many of these intellectuals and artists stayed in New York City, where Columbia University would become the main hub of Spanish activity, an institution which Carmen de Zulueta would dub "Spain on the Hudson." Columbia was home to the linguist Tomás Navarro Tomás — director of the National Library during the war and a collaborator in the rescue of the national bibliographical heritage — and the poet Francisco García Lorca (brother of Federico). Margarita Ucelay, the writer Gloria Giner de los Ríos and her daughter Laura de los Ríos, the future wife of Francisco, were also teachers there. The poet Miguel Pizarro Zambrano (Maria Zambrano's cousin), the writer and plastic artist Eugenio F. Granell, the poets Joaquin Casalduero and Ernesto Guerra da Cal — professors at New York University — and the poet Bernardo Clariana also lived and taught Spanish there. Many other Spanish teachers and writers went to other prestigious universities in the East, such as Vassar College (New York state), where Pilar de Madariaga and Soledad Salinas, the poet's daughter, taught; Princeton, where Francisco Ayala, Américo Castro and Vicente Llorens taught; Rutgers (New Jersey), where the poet Marina Romero directed the Spanish Department; and institutions in Massachusetts such as Wellesley — Pedro Salinas, Jorge Guillén and his daughter Teresa Guillé — and Mount Holyoke College — Luis Cernuda and Concha de Albornoz — among others.

Another important focal point for the Spanish exiles, as well as for those Spaniards who arrived some decades later, was the Pacific coast. Some of the notable Spanish writers and intellectuals who taught at universities in California at various points include José Rubia Barcia, José Fernández Montesinos, Joaquín Casalduero, Carlos Blanco Aguinaga, Concha Zardoya and Ricardo Gullón. In the Southwest, the writers Ramón J. Sender and Ángel González taught in New Mexico, and Antonio Sánchez Barbudo taught in Texas. In the Midwest, Hispanists had a significant presence in Illinois, where the linguist Joan Coromines and the poets Concha Zardoya and Ana María Martínez Sagi taught for some time, as well as Minnesota and Wisconsin, where the poet Arturo Serrano Plaja taught.

But the most important center for Hispanism in the US in the 20th century was the Spanish School at Middlebury College in Vermont, a sophisticated center of cultural learning that included all types of Spanish activities, which the poet Pedro Salinas once dubbed "the Second Magdalena" in reference to the famous summer courses in Santander that managed to bring Hispanism together before the war. Inaugurated in 1917 and directed for several years by Juan Centeno, the Spanish School and its summer courses became one of the most important enclaves for Hispanism at the time. For years, many of these exiled teachers went there to teach and meet, establishing connections with other Hispanists who had remained in Spain, as well as with American, European and Hispanic American Hispanists.

Most of these teachers went on to become professors and heads of the Spanish departments at their respective universities — including several women, such as Pilar de Madariaga at Vassar, Marina Romero at Rutgers and Justina Ruiz de Conde at Wellesley. Within their departments, many of them created magazines on Hispanic philology, such as the *Revista Hispánica Moderna* (founded by Onís in 1934 at Columbia) and *Mester* (founded by Rubia Barcia in 1970 at UCLA). Many also won prestigious American prizes and were awarded fellowships such as the Bollingen Prize (Francisco García Lorca, Juan Larrea) and the Guggenheim Fellowship (Agustí Bartra, Juan Larrea, Rosa Chacel, José Ferrater Mora, José Francisco Cirre, et al.). These Hispanists of the mid-20th century not only nourished American universities — they also founded Hispanism-related literary awards, bookstores, publishing houses and magazines, such as the New York-based Ibérica Publishing Company and its magazine, *Ibérica: por la Libertad* (founded by Victoria Kent), and *Mensaje* (a publishing house and magazine, founded by Eloy Vaquero and Odón Betanzos Palacios, both Andalusians). Most of these publishing operations, as well as the main Hispanic gatherings, were located in the area of Columbia University and around 14th Street in Manhattan, NYC, which was known as "Little Spain" ever since the arrival of the first waves of Spanish immigrants at the beginning of the 20th century. And finally, they founded Hispanic institutions and associations, including the Ibero-American Writers and Poets Guild of New York (*Círculo de Escritores y Poetas Iberoamericanos, CEPI*) and the North American Academy of the Spanish Language (*Academia Norteamericana de la Lengua Española*, ANLE), both of which were created in collaboration with Hispanists from Hispanic American countries — and, the latter, by famous exiles such as Corominas, Ferrater Mora, Guillén and Navarro Tomás, also in collaboration with American Hispanists.

The legacy and imprint of these mid- and late-20th-century Hispanists, especially that of the exiles — the largest group — has remained in the American university system for years through their disciples. The Eurocentric and more traditional philological view of some of them would eventually conflict with the Americanist approach promoted by other factions in the Spanish departments. Overcoming these circumstances, two main trends can currently be seen in these departments. The first trend is governed by the east and west coast axes of the US, where decades ago Hispanism began to be decentralized as a result of the arrival of new exiles, Hispanic Americans, who would progressively occupy a predominant place in the departments; today, we talk of Iberian or Peninsular studies and of Latin American studies, which fall under the umbrella of Transatlantic studies. The second trend concerns a peripheral Hispanism, which broadens the object of study of Peninsularism through cultural studies, focusing on gender and queer theory, comics, popular literature, etc. Today, some of the most innovative proposals of international peninsular Hispanism arrive from these universities, through Spanish, American and Hispanic American researchers.

SCIENCE

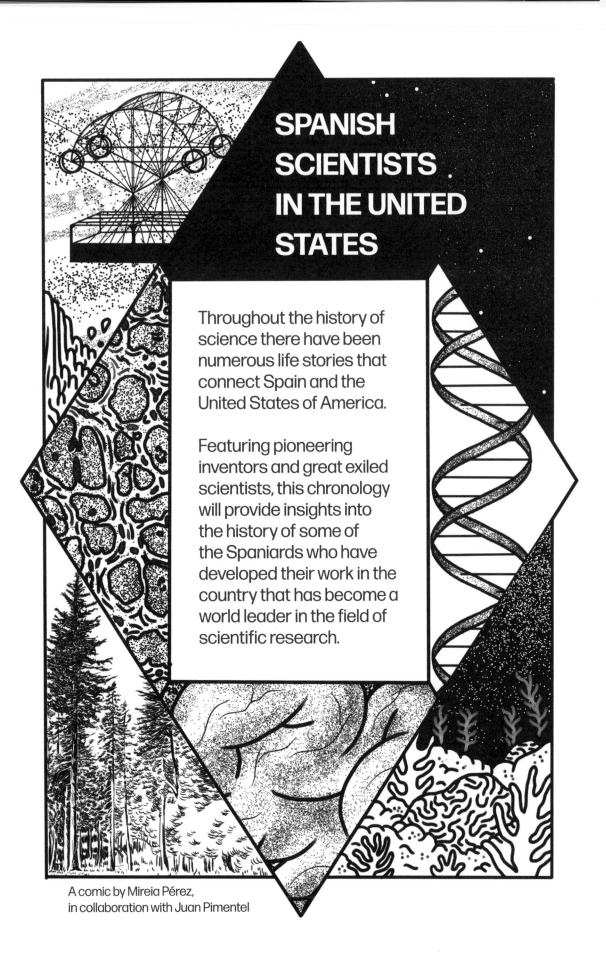

SPANISH SCIENTISTS IN THE UNITED STATES

Throughout the history of science there have been numerous life stories that connect Spain and the United States of America.

Featuring pioneering inventors and great exiled scientists, this chronology will provide insights into the history of some of the Spaniards who have developed their work in the country that has become a world leader in the field of scientific research.

A comic by Mireia Pérez, in collaboration with Juan Pimentel

PIONEERING INVENTIONS

We owe the existence of the mechanical calculator largely to **Ramón Verea**. This great engineer and inventor from Galicia was also a progressive, anti-slavery writer. He lived in New York between 1865 and 1895. His prototype was more successful than others because it could handle multiplication.

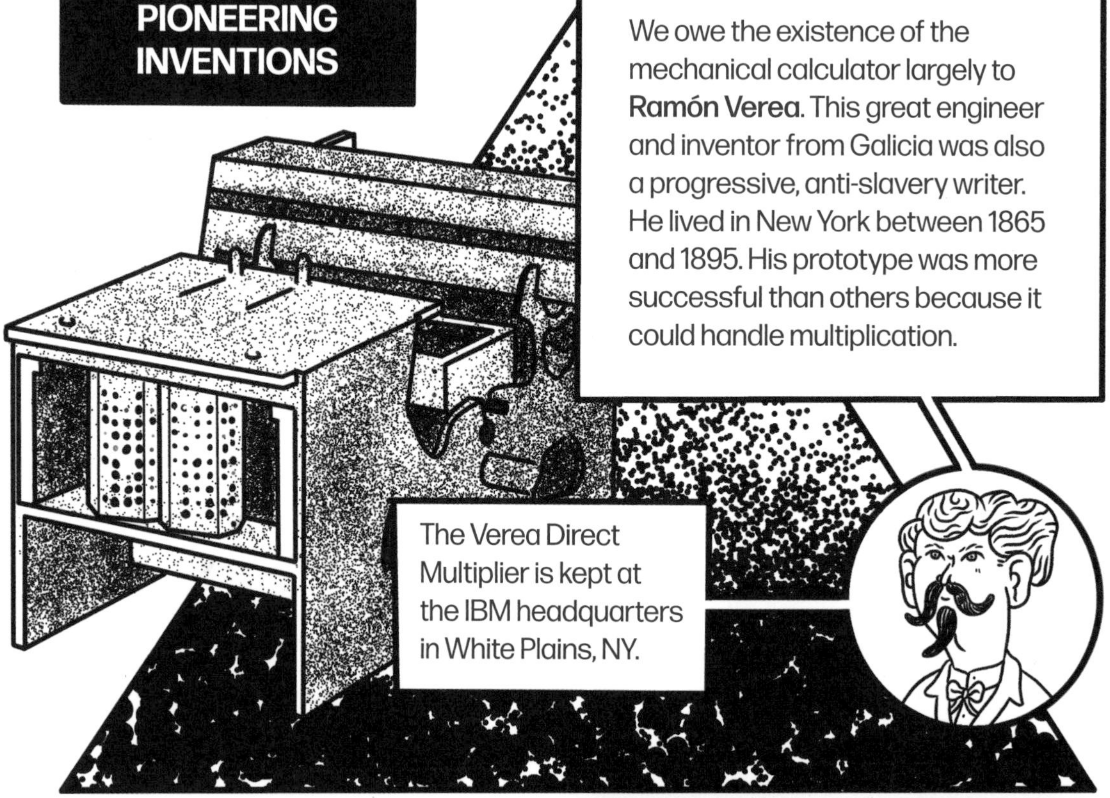

The Verea Direct Multiplier is kept at the IBM headquarters in White Plains, NY.

The young electrician from La Mancha, **Mónico Sánchez**, emigrated to New York in 1904, where he studied engineering while learning English. He invented a successful portable device for X-rays and high frequency currents and was employed by the Collins Wireless Telephone Company.

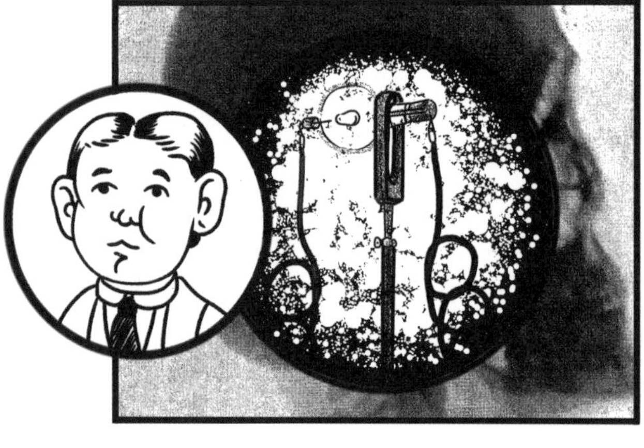

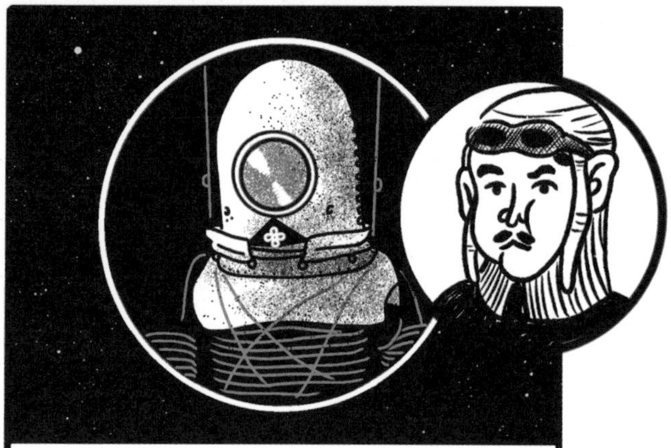

Emilio Herrera Linares was an aviator, military engineer and President of the Spanish Republic in exile. In 1935, he designed the first space suit for stratospheric flights, a precursor to the modern space suit that NASA would develop years later.

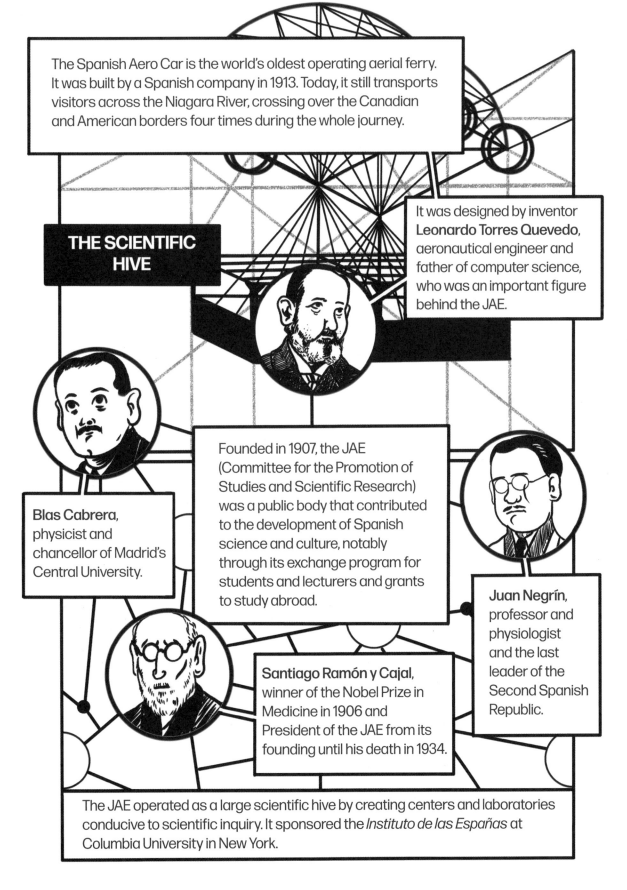

The Spanish Aero Car is the world's oldest operating aerial ferry. It was built by a Spanish company in 1913. Today, it still transports visitors across the Niagara River, crossing over the Canadian and American borders four times during the whole journey.

THE SCIENTIFIC HIVE

It was designed by inventor **Leonardo Torres Quevedo**, aeronautical engineer and father of computer science, who was an important figure behind the JAE.

Blas Cabrera, physicist and chancellor of Madrid's Central University.

Founded in 1907, the JAE (Committee for the Promotion of Studies and Scientific Research) was a public body that contributed to the development of Spanish science and culture, notably through its exchange program for students and lecturers and grants to study abroad.

Juan Negrín, professor and physiologist and the last leader of the Second Spanish Republic.

Santiago Ramón y Cajal, winner of the Nobel Prize in Medicine in 1906 and President of the JAE from its founding until his death in 1934.

The JAE operated as a large scientific hive by creating centers and laboratories conducive to scientific inquiry. It sponsored the *Instituto de las Españas* at Columbia University in New York.

The Laboratory of Physical Research (LIF, as per its Spanish acronym) of the JAE, led by Blas Cabrera, helped put Spanish physical sciences on the map of the international scientific community.

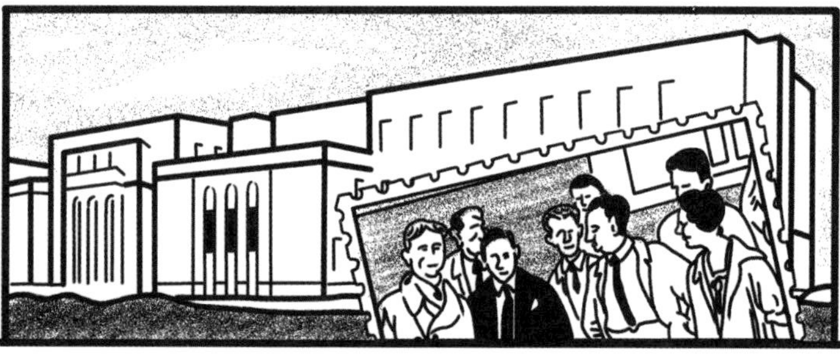

In 1923, **José Castillejo**, Secretary of the JAE, negotiated with the Rockefeller Foundation to fund a building to house the LIF. The so-called Rockefeller Institute was built between 1926 and 1932 and is now the headquarters of the Rocasolano Institute of Chemistry and Physics of the CSIC (The Spanish National Research Council).

REPRESSION AND EXILE

The JAE was dismantled in 1939 under Franco's regime and re-founded as the Spanish National Research Council (CSIC, as per its Spanish acronym). Many of its members were purged and went into exile, some of them to the US.

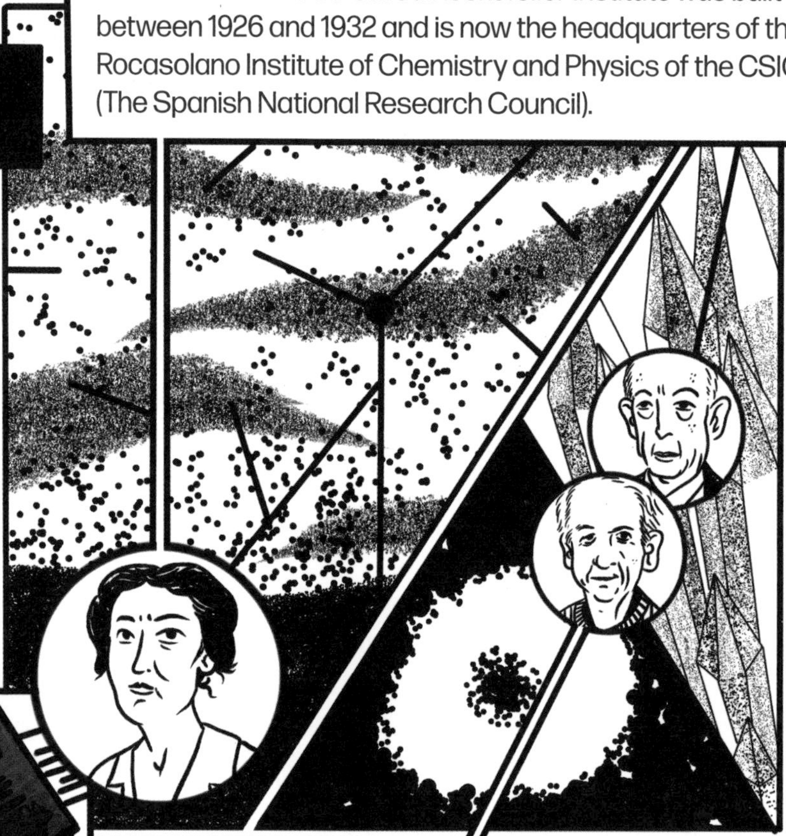

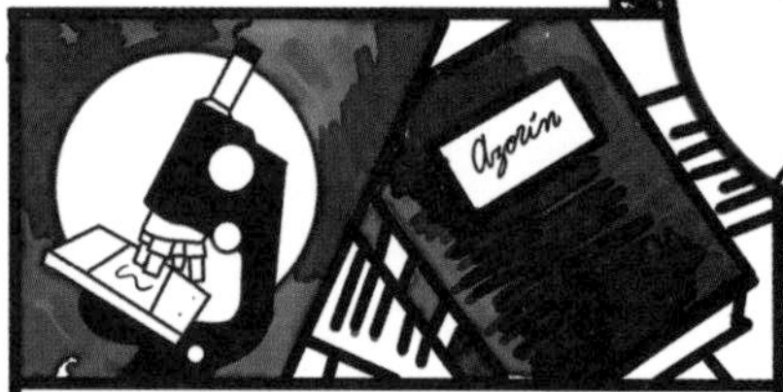
Azorín

Pilar de Madariaga Rojo, an LIF chemist who studied at Vassar College thanks to the JAE, went back to New York during her exile. Rebuilding her career, she later became the head of the Department of Hispanic Studies.

Blas Cabrera's son, **Nicolás Cabrera**, completed his studies in psychics abroad and became an important researcher in the field of crystal growth. He was hired by the University of Virginia in 1952. His grandson, **Blas Cabrera Navarro**, became an American citizen and a physicist. Since the 1980s, he has studied the origins of the Big Bang and dark matter.

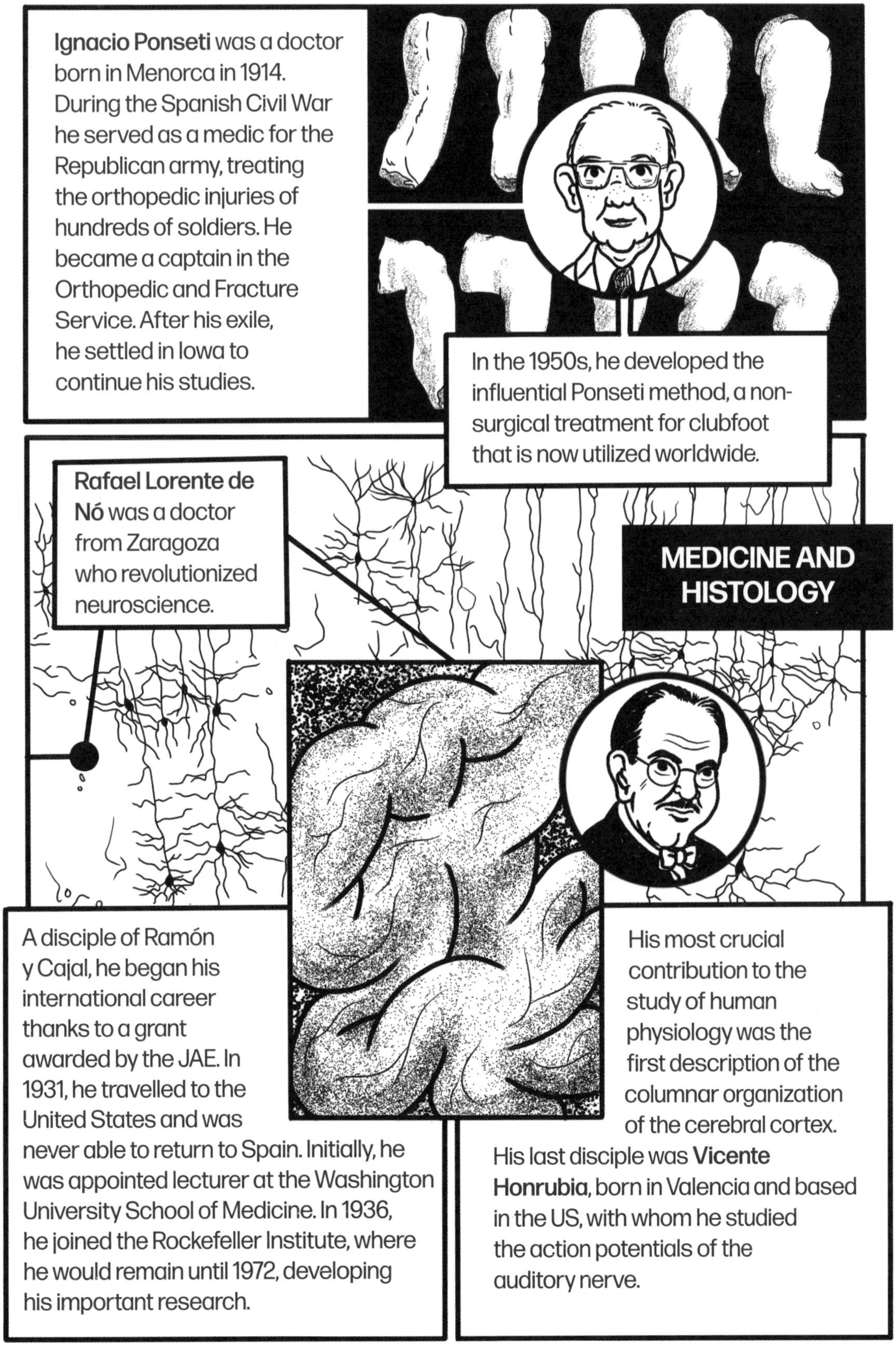

Ignacio Ponseti was a doctor born in Menorca in 1914. During the Spanish Civil War he served as a medic for the Republican army, treating the orthopedic injuries of hundreds of soldiers. He became a captain in the Orthopedic and Fracture Service. After his exile, he settled in Iowa to continue his studies.

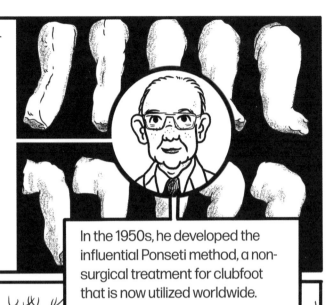

In the 1950s, he developed the influential Ponseti method, a non-surgical treatment for clubfoot that is now utilized worldwide.

Rafael Lorente de Nó was a doctor from Zaragoza who revolutionized neuroscience.

MEDICINE AND HISTOLOGY

A disciple of Ramón y Cajal, he began his international career thanks to a grant awarded by the JAE. In 1931, he travelled to the United States and was never able to return to Spain. Initially, he was appointed lecturer at the Washington University School of Medicine. In 1936, he joined the Rockefeller Institute, where he would remain until 1972, developing his important research.

His most crucial contribution to the study of human physiology was the first description of the columnar organization of the cerebral cortex.

His last disciple was Vicente Honrubia, born in Valencia and based in the US, with whom he studied the action potentials of the auditory nerve.

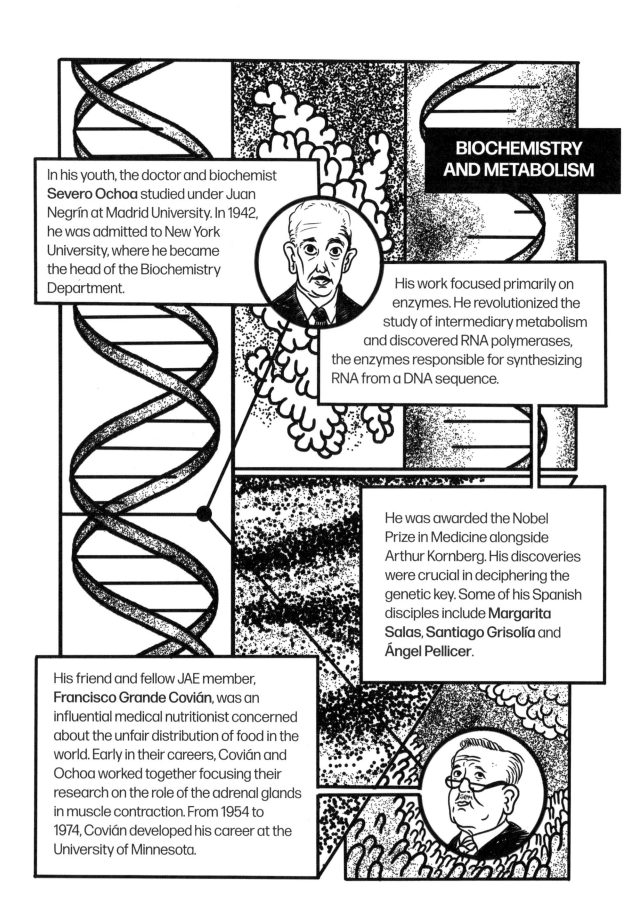

BIOCHEMISTRY AND METABOLISM

In his youth, the doctor and biochemist **Severo Ochoa** studied under Juan Negrín at Madrid University. In 1942, he was admitted to New York University, where he became the head of the Biochemistry Department.

His work focused primarily on enzymes. He revolutionized the study of intermediary metabolism and discovered RNA polymerases, the enzymes responsible for synthesizing RNA from a DNA sequence.

He was awarded the Nobel Prize in Medicine alongside Arthur Kornberg. His discoveries were crucial in deciphering the genetic key. Some of his Spanish disciples include **Margarita Salas**, **Santiago Grisolía** and **Ángel Pellicer**.

His friend and fellow JAE member, **Francisco Grande Covián**, was an influential medical nutritionist concerned about the unfair distribution of food in the world. Early in their careers, Covián and Ochoa worked together focusing their research on the role of the adrenal glands in muscle contraction. From 1954 to 1974, Covián developed his career at the University of Minnesota.

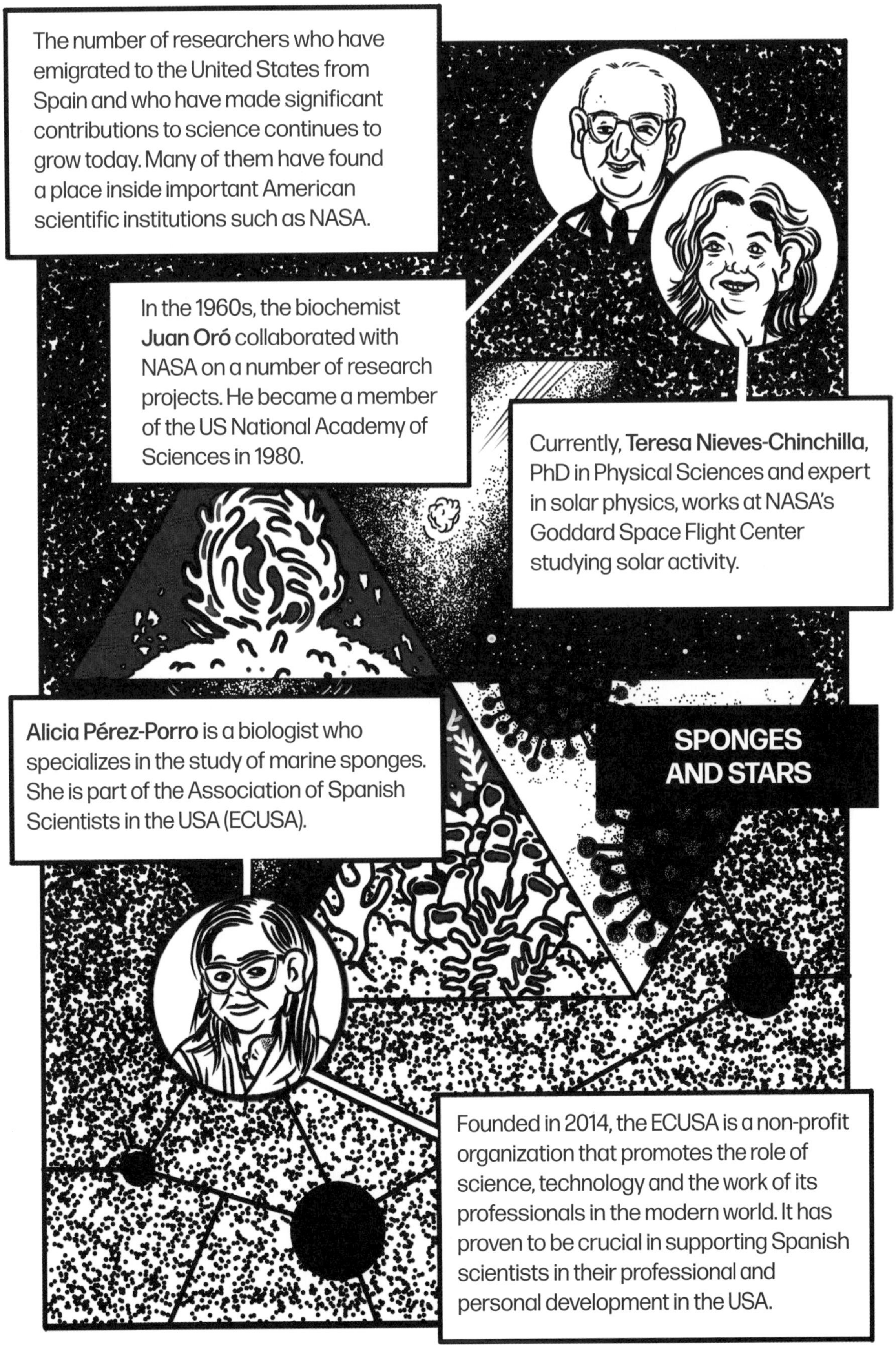
The number of researchers who have emigrated to the United States from Spain and who have made significant contributions to science continues to grow today. Many of them have found a place inside important American scientific institutions such as NASA.
In the 1960s, the biochemist **Juan Oró** collaborated with NASA on a number of research projects. He became a member of the US National Academy of Sciences in 1980.
Currently, **Teresa Nieves-Chinchilla**, PhD in Physical Sciences and expert in solar physics, works at NASA's Goddard Space Flight Center studying solar activity.
Alicia Pérez-Porro is a biologist who specializes in the study of marine sponges. She is part of the Association of Spanish Scientists in the USA (ECUSA).
SPONGES AND STARS
Founded in 2014, the ECUSA is a non-profit organization that promotes the role of science, technology and the work of its professionals in the modern world. It has proven to be crucial in supporting Spanish scientists in their professional and personal development in the USA.

Spanish Scientists in the USA

Juan Pimentel

PROFESSOR OF HISTORY, SPANISH NATIONAL RESEARCH COUNCIL

IN A RECENT INTERVIEW, psychiatrist Luis Rojas Marcos talked about the effects of optimism on health, a theory that has been backed by scientific data and which is sure to be popular in the US. Born in Seville in 1943, Rojas Marcos has lived in New York since 1968, where he was head of the Mental Health Services for many years. In the Big Apple he promoted a project called HELP (Homeless Emergency Liasion Project), which has been replicated in many countries. He also played an important role in the aftermath of 9/11 in the treatment of trauma, anxiety and other mental illnesses.

Years ago, in 1835, another Spaniard, Ramón de la Sagra, botanist, economist, politician and liberal writer, made a journey through New York, Philadelphia, Connecticut, Baltimore, Boston and, finally, Niagara Falls. The following year, he published *Cinco meses en los Estados Unidos de la América del Norte* (Five months in the United States of North America), a Tocqueville-style book in which he reflected on the achievements and virtues of this young nation, its commitment to freedom and group work, the philanthropy he saw in its hospitals, prisons, mental asylums and schools.

The hope for a better future is ingrained in the history of the United States. Indeed, the Spanish scientists who emigrated or were exiled to this "promised land" sought to build a better future for themselves as well as to improve the standards of living for all mankind.

Challenging the stereotype of a nation with little inclination to science, several pioneering inventions were made by Spaniards. One of the first mechanical calculators, for example, was devised by Ramón Verea, an abolitionist engineer and writer who also lived in New York between 1865 and 1895. His mechanical computer is kept at IBM's headquarters in White Plains, NY. In turn, Leonardo Torres Quevedo (1852–1936) was one of the giants of aerial and automatic engineering, known for designing the Spanish Aero Car, which still transports visitors in Niagara Falls, the final destination on his American journey. He can also be considered one of the fathers of computing. Between 1895 and 1914, Torres Quevedo invented some of the first analogue and electromagnetic calculation machines, as well as the telekino, a predecessor of the remote control. Another pioneer of wireless telecommunications was Mónico Sánchez, who emigrated to the US in 1904, where he designed a portable X-ray machine and was hired by the Collins Wireless Telephone Company.

In 1935, Emilio Herrera Linares, an aviator and engineer who became President of the Second Spanish Republic in exile, designed the stratonautical space suit that NASA developed in the following decades. One of his disciples, Manuel Casajust, who worked at NASA in the days of Apollo 11, once related that when Neil Armstrong returned from his historic journey in 1969, the astronaut told him that if it had not been for his master's invention, he would have never reached the moon. Years later, Miguel López-Alegría, who was raised in the United States and was an American citizen, became the first Spanish-born astronaut. His first space flight took place in 1995.

Science is a group activity that brings together thousands of professionals in a collaborative setting. The scientists working at NASA and other American scientific institutions come from a variety of backgrounds, because innovative countries seek out talent and don't care where it comes from.

Just as American cinema and the American intellectual sphere were enriched by many exiles during the terrible Nazi era, just as the crew of the Mayflower found a home in America, science in the US has always recruited the best minds and undertaken the boldest projects. Some of them were Spanish, individuals who fled the Spanish Civil War (1936–1939) and the dictatorship of General Franco (1939–1975). Others emigrated in the hope of finding better opportunities in the US. Many were linked to the *Junta para Ampliación de Estudios* (JAE, the Committee for the Promotion of Studies and Scientific Research), a scientific institution created in 1907 and led by José Castillejo and Santiago Ramón y Cajal. Dissolved after the Spanish Civil War, the organization was re-founded in 1939 as the *Consejo Superior de Investigaciones Científicas* (CSIC, the Spanish National Research Council), now the largest public research body in Spain.

This was the case of Rafael Lorente de Nó (1902–1990), a disciple of Ramón y Cajal who emigrated to the United States in 1931. He went on to have a brilliant career in the field of cerebral histology (neural tissues), first in Missouri, then at the Rockefeller Institute in New York and finally in Tucson. He explored the region of the hippocampus where the mysterious relationship between smell and memory occurs. He also investigated the electrical recording of neurons, thus broadening the field of electrophysiology. He is considered one of the fathers of neurobiology and many consider his research to be worthy of a Nobel Prize.

One Spaniard who did win a Nobel Prize was Severo Ochoa (1905–1993). A biochemist, Ochoa fled Spain at the beginning of the Spanish Civil War and settled in the US in 1940, living in St. Louis and New York and ultimately becoming an American citizen. He made one of the most fruitful discoveries in the history of molecular biology when he managed to isolate an enzyme that acted as an intermediary between proteins and DNA and was also capable of synthesizing RNA *in vitro*. Isolating that enzyme, the polynucleotide phosphorylase (PNPase), made it possible to create synthetic polynucleotides, which ultimately were fundamental to the development of genetics. This discovery earned him the Nobel Prize for Physiology and Medicine in 1959 (jointly with Arthur Kornberg). Ochoa also had several Spanish disciples, who either lived in the US or were frequent visitors, such as Santiago Grisolía (a great scholar of certain metabolism processes), Margarita Salas (researcher of polymerases, the enzymes involved in DNA replication) and Ángel Pellicer (a leading oncologist).

One of Ochoa's notable colleagues in the golden years of the JAE and its *Residencia de Estudiantes* (Residential College) was Francisco Grande Covián (1909–1995), an influential nutritionist and founder of the current studies on dietetics. He lived in the US for 20 years and only returned to Spain after the death of the dictator.

Juan Oró (1923–2004) is another Spanish biochemist who spent more than half of his life in the US. He carried out his research in Houston, at whose university he founded the Department of Biochemical and Biophysical Sciences. Oró excelled in a discipline as fascinating as astrobiology and the study of the origin of life. He sought to answer the question of whether life was possible on Mars or elsewhere in the universe. Through his studies, he helped create the panspermia theory, which suggests that life is distributed throughout the universe and that it arrived on Earth thanks to the comets that struck our planet.

Science concerns everything that has passed and all that is new, from theoretical matters to more immediate problems. Ignacio Ponseti (1914–2009), a Spanish doctor exiled in the US, was able to develop a non-surgical method for treating clubfoot at the University of Iowa, a method which is now widely spread throughout the world. The specialty of Joan Massagué (b. 1953), pharmacist and biochemist, also focuses on alleviating suffering: oncology. Massagué moved to Providence in 1982 to work at Brown University. He later moved to the University of Massachusetts and currently works at the Howard Hughes Medical Institute, a non-profit philanthropic organization and one of the world's leading medical foundations. Massagué is now one of the world's leading specialists in cancer and metastatic reproduction.

The passion for science is contagious. It inspires one scientist after another, like music among musicians or sport among sportsmen. Sometimes, it's not unusual for this enthusiasm to be passed on through bloodlines as well. Two families of progressively-Americanized Spanish scientists are a good example of this.

Perhaps the most outstanding Spanish physicist of the first half of the 20th century was (along with Miguel Catalán, a great spectroscopist who also lived for some years in the US) Blas Cabrera (1878–1945). He was head of the Laboratory of Physical Research (LIF, as per its Spanish acronym), founded in 1910 within the JAE, an institute that attracted the attention of the Rockefeller Foundation, which shortly thereafter supported the creation of an Institute of Physical and Chemical Sciences in the famous *Edificio Rockefeller* (literally, the Rockefeller Building, which today belongs to the CSIC). Cabrera, who hosted Einstein on his visit to Madrid and was a friend of Marie Curie and Niels Bohr, went into exile in Mexico after the Spanish Civil War; however, his son, Nicolás Cabrera (1913–1989), also a physicist, settled in the US. At the University of Virginia, Nicolás became one of the greatest experts in crystal growth. In turn, his son, Blas Cabrera Navarro (b. 1946), who was born when his parents and grandparents were in exile in Paris, pursued his scientific career at Stanford University. As the third generation of a great family of physicists, he discovered the basic unit of magnetism, the magnetic monopoles, which are the elementary particles that explain the Big Bang and dark matter. This subject of study links him to a certain extent to Juan Oró's research on the origin of life. The fields of American quantum physics and astrobiology bear Spanish traces in their paths.

Four generations make up the Álvarez family. Asturian-born Luis Fernández Álvarez (1853–1937) emigrated first to Cuba and then to the US. He studied medicine at Cooper Medical

College (now Stanford University) and then moved to Hawaii. He worked in leper colonies both there and in California and developed a method for diagnosing tuberculoid or macular leprosy. There were always epidemics. And there were also always men and women who were committed to fighting them, alleviating their consequences and eventually eradicating them. His son, Walter C. Álvarez (1884–1978), was a very popular doctor among the American middle class and one of the forerunners in the depathologization of homosexuality. He in turn had a son, Luis Walter Álvarez (1911–1988), a physicist and a professor at Berkeley and MIT who worked on the Manhattan Project of the Los Alamos National Laboratory, which focused on the development of the atomic bomb during the Second World War. Luis Walter Álvarez designed one of the first particle accelerators, invented the liquid hydrogen bubble chamber and experimented in several fields of nuclear physics, cosmic rays and high energies. He was a brilliant and versatile man who received the Nobel Prize in Physics in 1968. In addition, he collaborated with his son Walter Álvarez (b. 1940), a renowned professor of geology at Berkeley with whom he postulated the famous theory that an asteroid impact caused the extinction of dinosaurs. Together they also developed a system to view inside the pyramids of Egypt using X-rays. An incredibly high achieving family made up of doctors, physicists and geologists, who fought diseases and changed the course of World War II and investigated the Earth's distant past. Science is truly a multifaceted, complex and creative activity.

Nowadays, quite a few Spanish scientists work in the US. Some of the leading lights among them are women. Teresa Nieves-Chinchilla, for example, is an astrophysicist who works at NASA's Heliophysics Science Division and gives scientific support to space probes that study the physical conditions of the sun. Alicia Pérez-Porro is a marine biologist specialized in the study of marine sponges. Until recently, she chaired the association of Spanish Scientists in the USA (ECUSA). Other members of ECUSA are Ana Fernández-Sesma and Elisabeth Diago Navarro, who both study viruses and other pathogens. The former is a professor of microbiology and infectious diseases at the Icahn School of Medicine at Mount Sinai in New York. The latter is a biologist who has participated in a recent annual expedition to Antarctica to study climate change known as Homeward Bound, an apt name when considering migrants and the Earth, our common home. Is there anything more urgent, more necessary and more beautiful than exploring nature, life itself in all its fragility as well as its determination to keep moving forward?

CINEMA

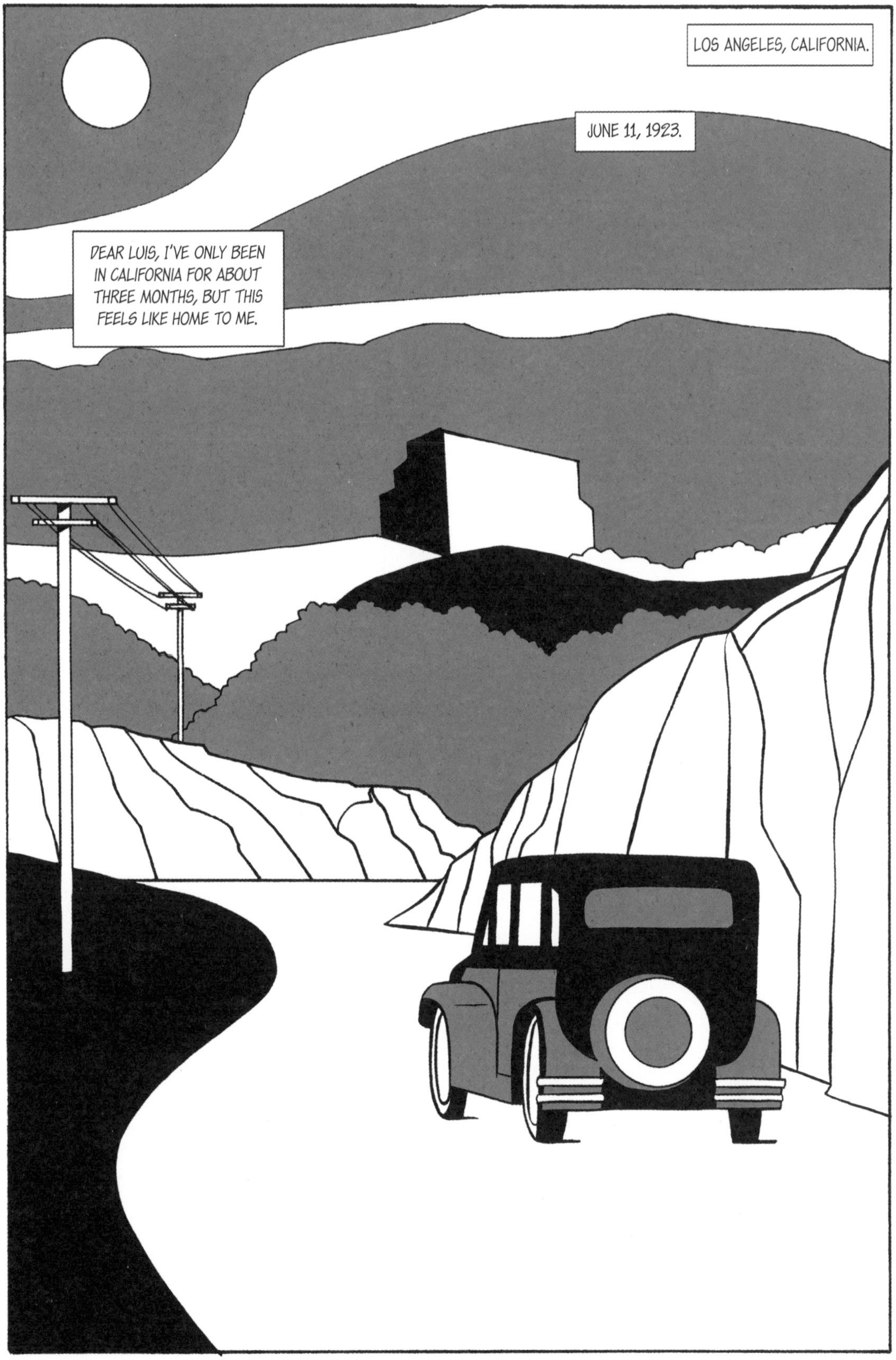
LOS ANGELES, CALIFORNIA.
JUNE 11, 1923.
DEAR LUIS, I'VE ONLY BEEN IN CALIFORNIA FOR ABOUT THREE MONTHS, BUT THIS FEELS LIKE HOME TO ME.

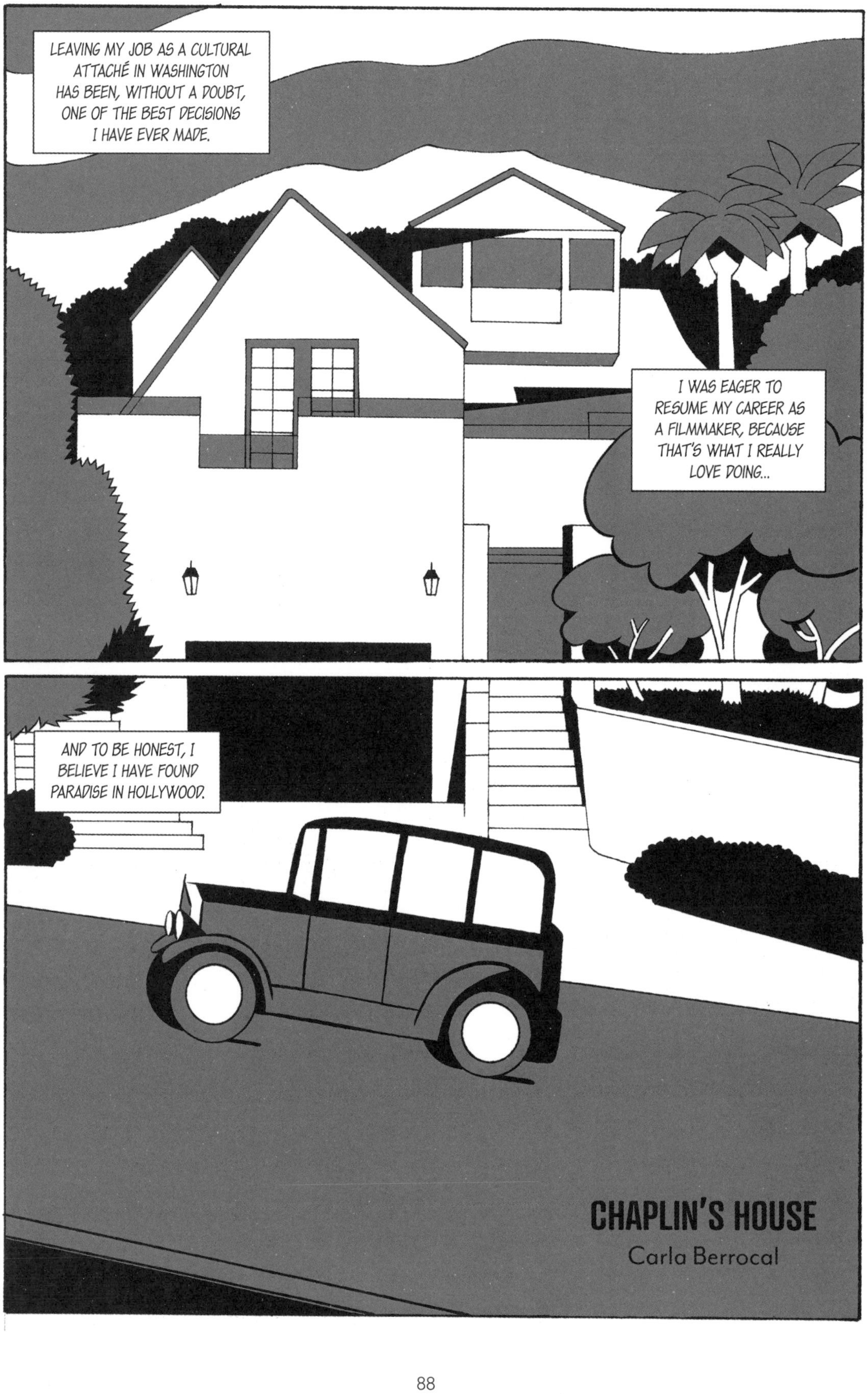
LEAVING MY JOB AS A CULTURAL ATTACHÉ IN WASHINGTON HAS BEEN, WITHOUT A DOUBT, ONE OF THE BEST DECISIONS I HAVE EVER MADE.
I WAS EAGER TO RESUME MY CAREER AS A FILMMAKER, BECAUSE THAT'S WHAT I REALLY LOVE DOING...
AND TO BE HONEST, I BELIEVE I HAVE FOUND PARADISE IN HOLLYWOOD.
CHAPLIN'S HOUSE
Carla Berrocal

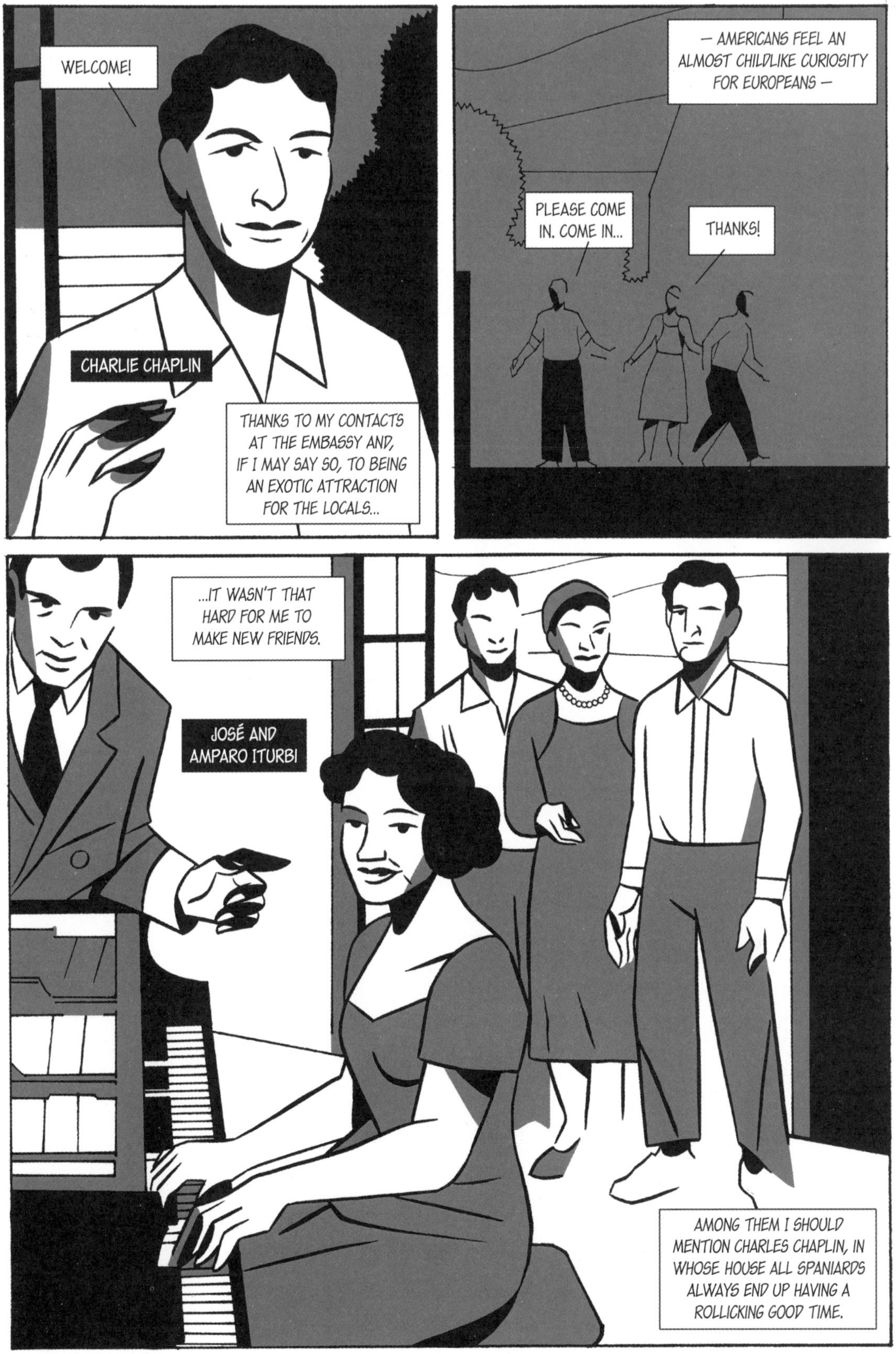
WELCOME!
CHARLIE CHAPLIN
THANKS TO MY CONTACTS AT THE EMBASSY AND, IF I MAY SAY SO, TO BEING AN EXOTIC ATTRACTION FOR THE LOCALS...
— AMERICANS FEEL AN ALMOST CHILDLIKE CURIOSITY FOR EUROPEANS —
PLEASE COME IN. COME IN...
THANKS!
...IT WASN'T THAT HARD FOR ME TO MAKE NEW FRIENDS.
JOSÉ AND AMPARO ITURBI
AMONG THEM I SHOULD MENTION CHARLES CHAPLIN, IN WHOSE HOUSE ALL SPANIARDS ALWAYS END UP HAVING A ROLLICKING GOOD TIME.

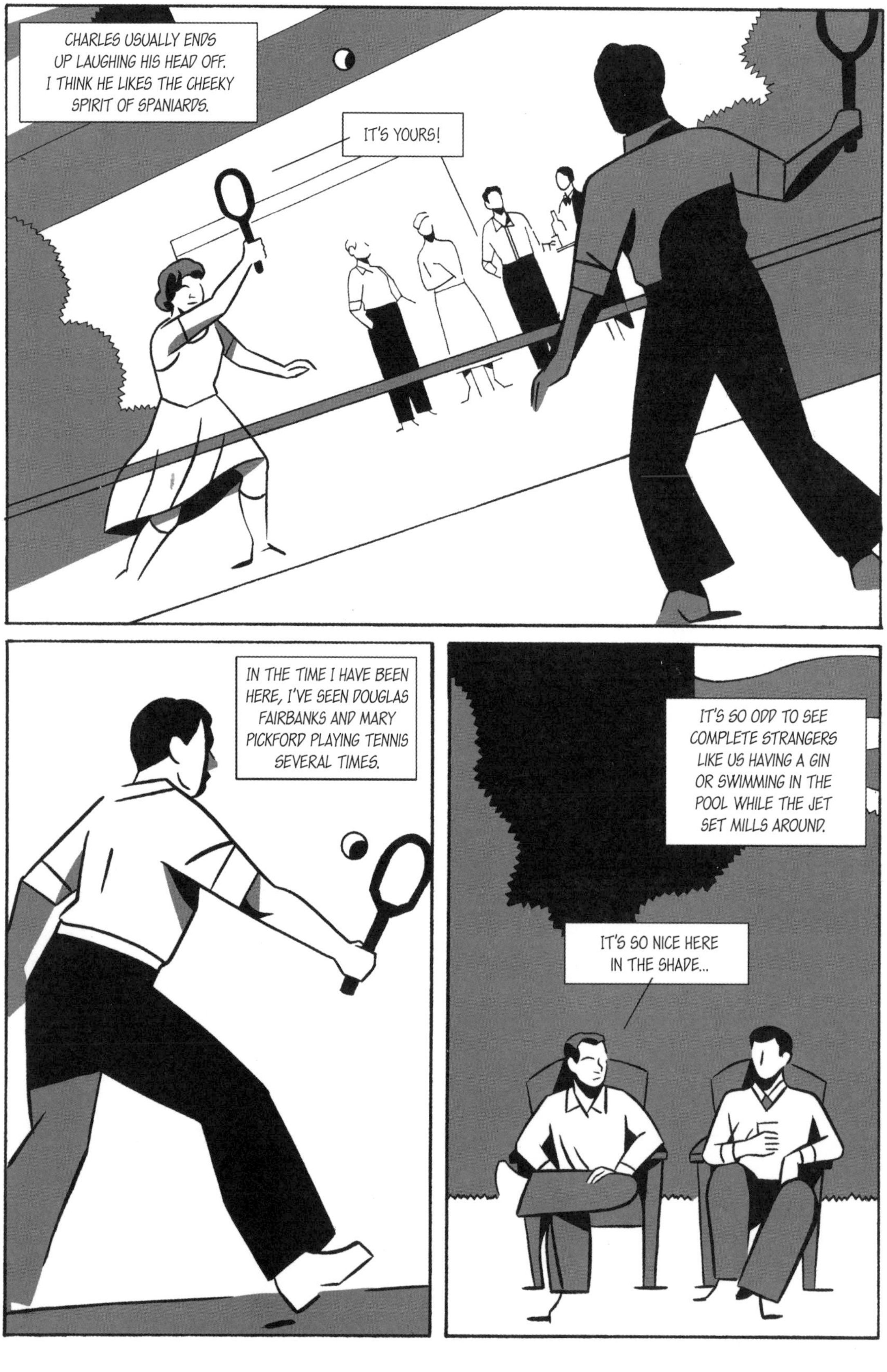
CHARLES USUALLY ENDS UP LAUGHING HIS HEAD OFF. I THINK HE LIKES THE CHEEKY SPIRIT OF SPANIARDS.
IT'S YOURS!
IN THE TIME I HAVE BEEN HERE, I'VE SEEN DOUGLAS FAIRBANKS AND MARY PICKFORD PLAYING TENNIS SEVERAL TIMES.
IT'S SO ODD TO SEE COMPLETE STRANGERS LIKE US HAVING A GIN OR SWIMMING IN THE POOL WHILE THE JET SET MILLS AROUND.
IT'S SO NICE HERE IN THE SHADE...

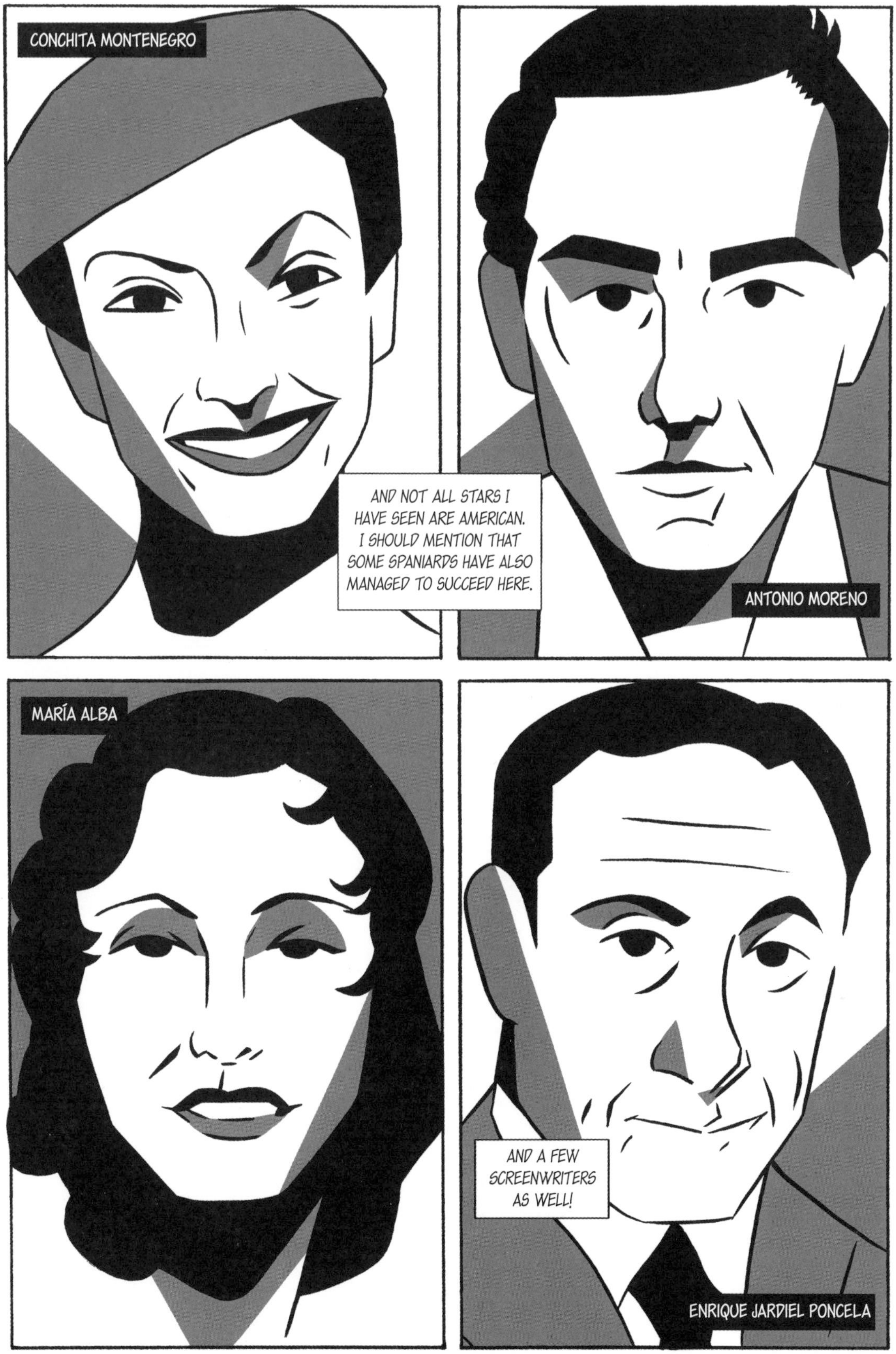
CONCHITA MONTENEGRO
AND NOT ALL STARS I HAVE SEEN ARE AMERICAN. I SHOULD MENTION THAT SOME SPANIARDS HAVE ALSO MANAGED TO SUCCEED HERE.
ANTONIO MORENO
MARÍA ALBA
AND A FEW SCREENWRITERS AS WELL!
ENRIQUE JARDIEL PONCELA

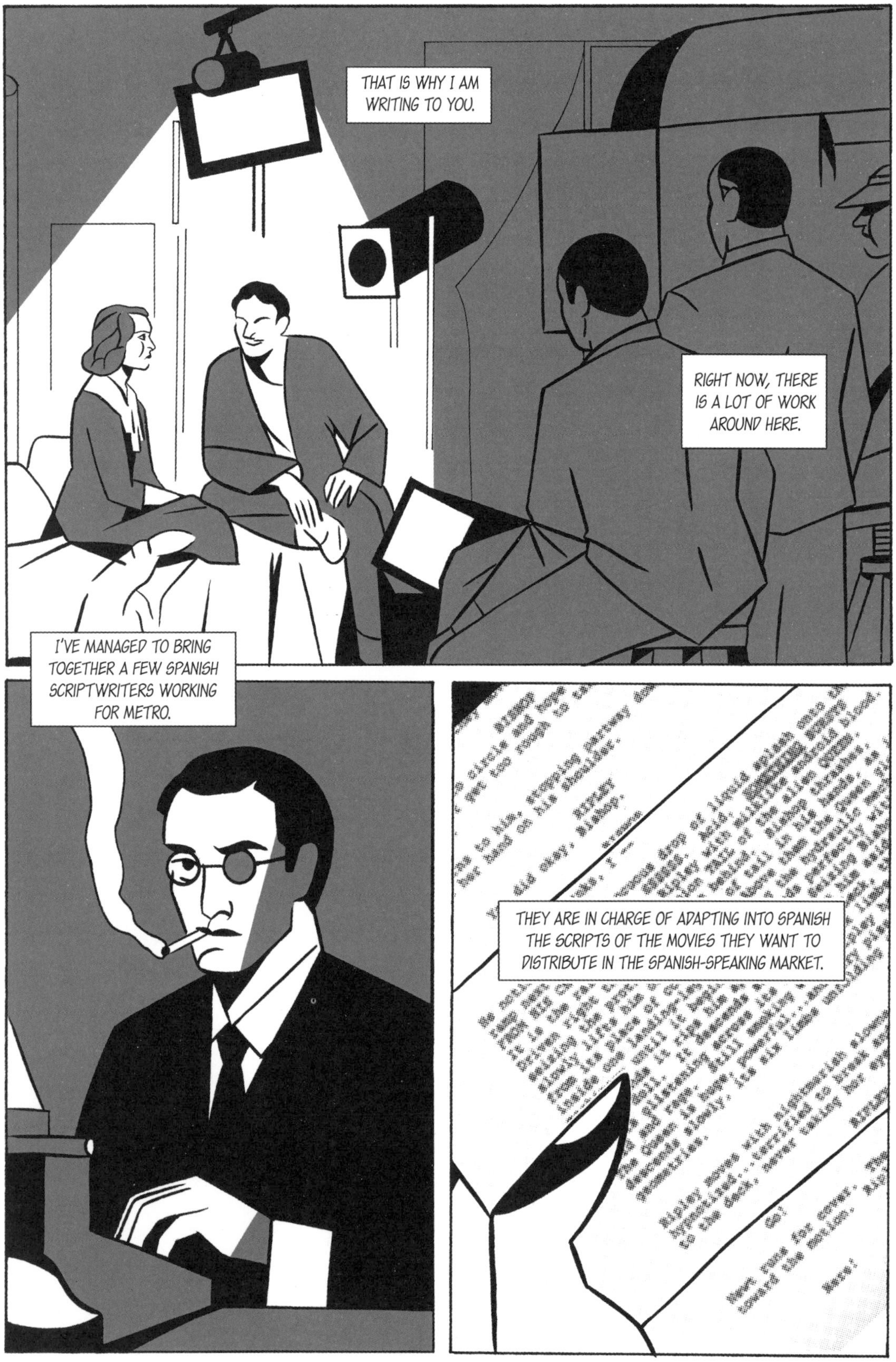
THAT IS WHY I AM WRITING TO YOU.
RIGHT NOW, THERE IS A LOT OF WORK AROUND HERE.
I'VE MANAGED TO BRING TOGETHER A FEW SPANISH SCRIPTWRITERS WORKING FOR METRO.
THEY ARE IN CHARGE OF ADAPTING INTO SPANISH THE SCRIPTS OF THE MOVIES THEY WANT TO DISTRIBUTE IN THE SPANISH-SPEAKING MARKET.

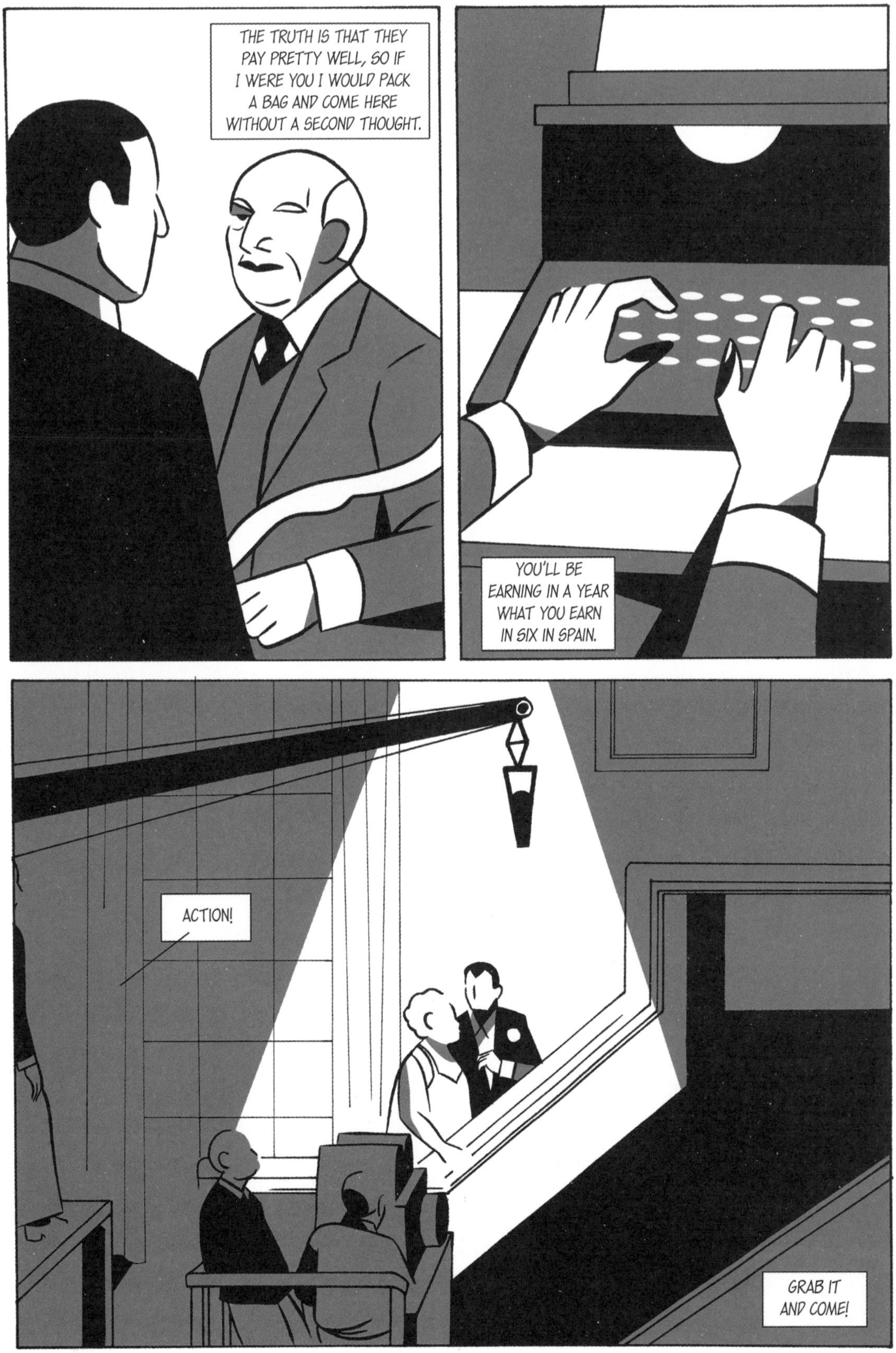
THE TRUTH IS THAT THEY PAY PRETTY WELL, SO IF I WERE YOU I WOULD PACK A BAG AND COME HERE WITHOUT A SECOND THOUGHT.
YOU'LL BE EARNING IN A YEAR WHAT YOU EARN IN SIX IN SPAIN.
ACTION!
GRAB IT AND COME!

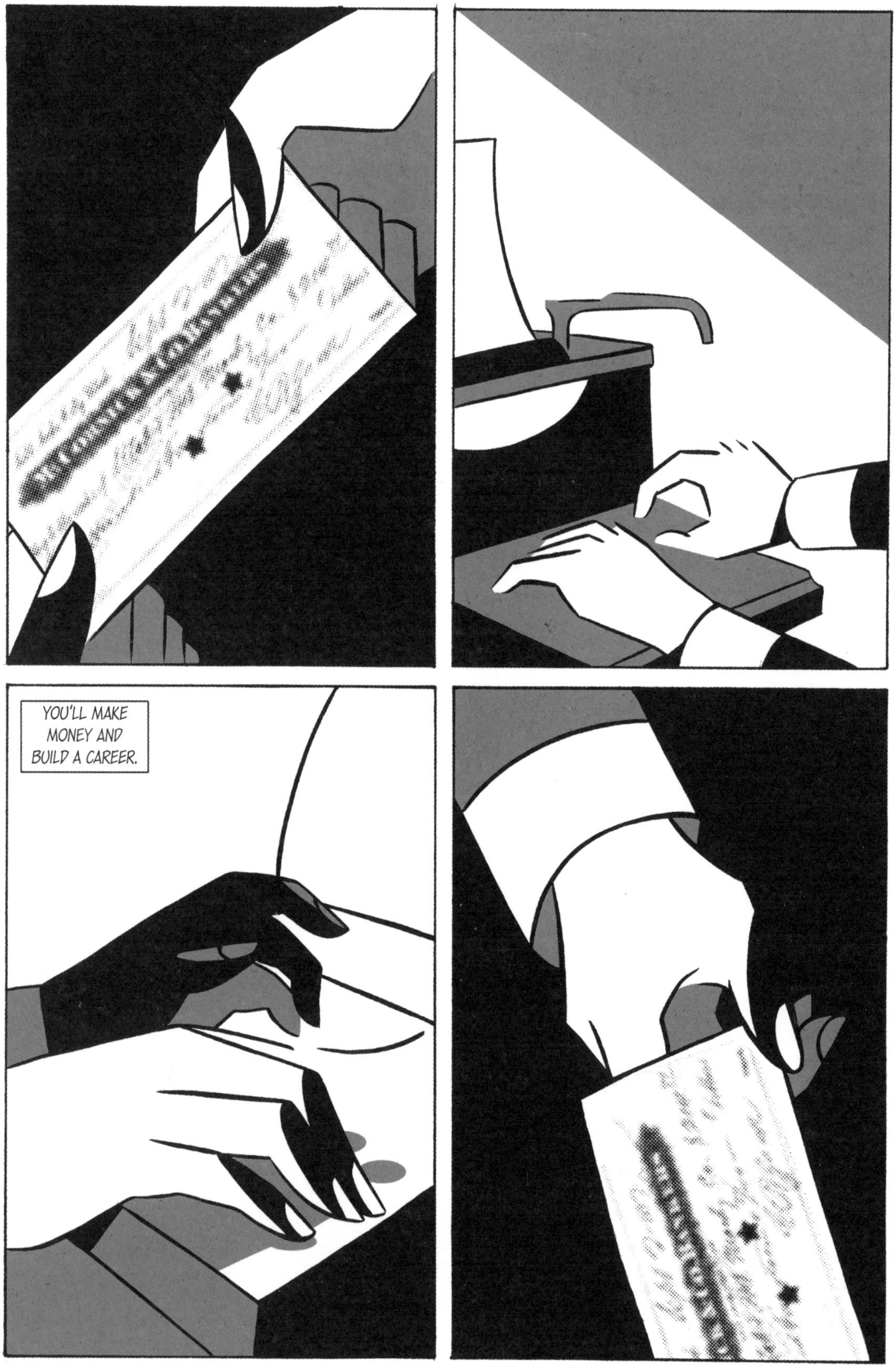
YOU'LL MAKE MONEY AND BUILD A CAREER.

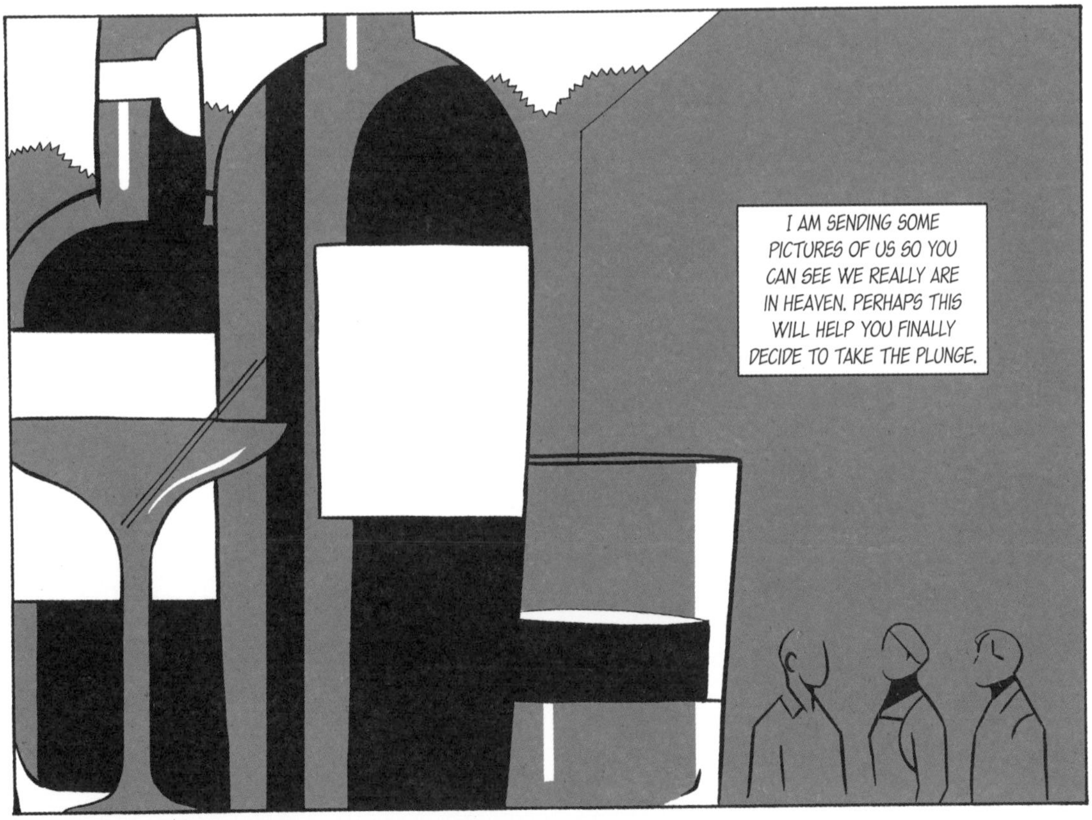
I AM SENDING SOME PICTURES OF US SO YOU CAN SEE WE REALLY ARE IN HEAVEN. PERHAPS THIS WILL HELP YOU FINALLY DECIDE TO TAKE THE PLUNGE.

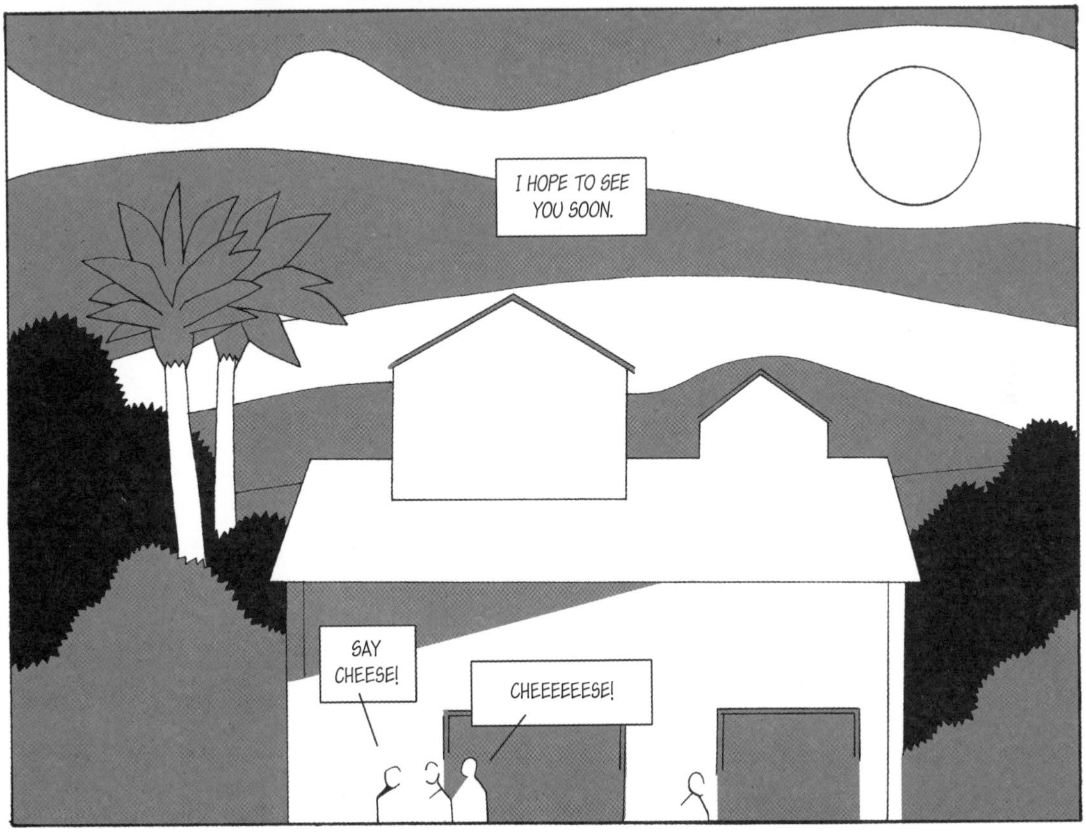
I HOPE TO SEE YOU SOON.
SAY CHEESE!
CHEEEEEESE!

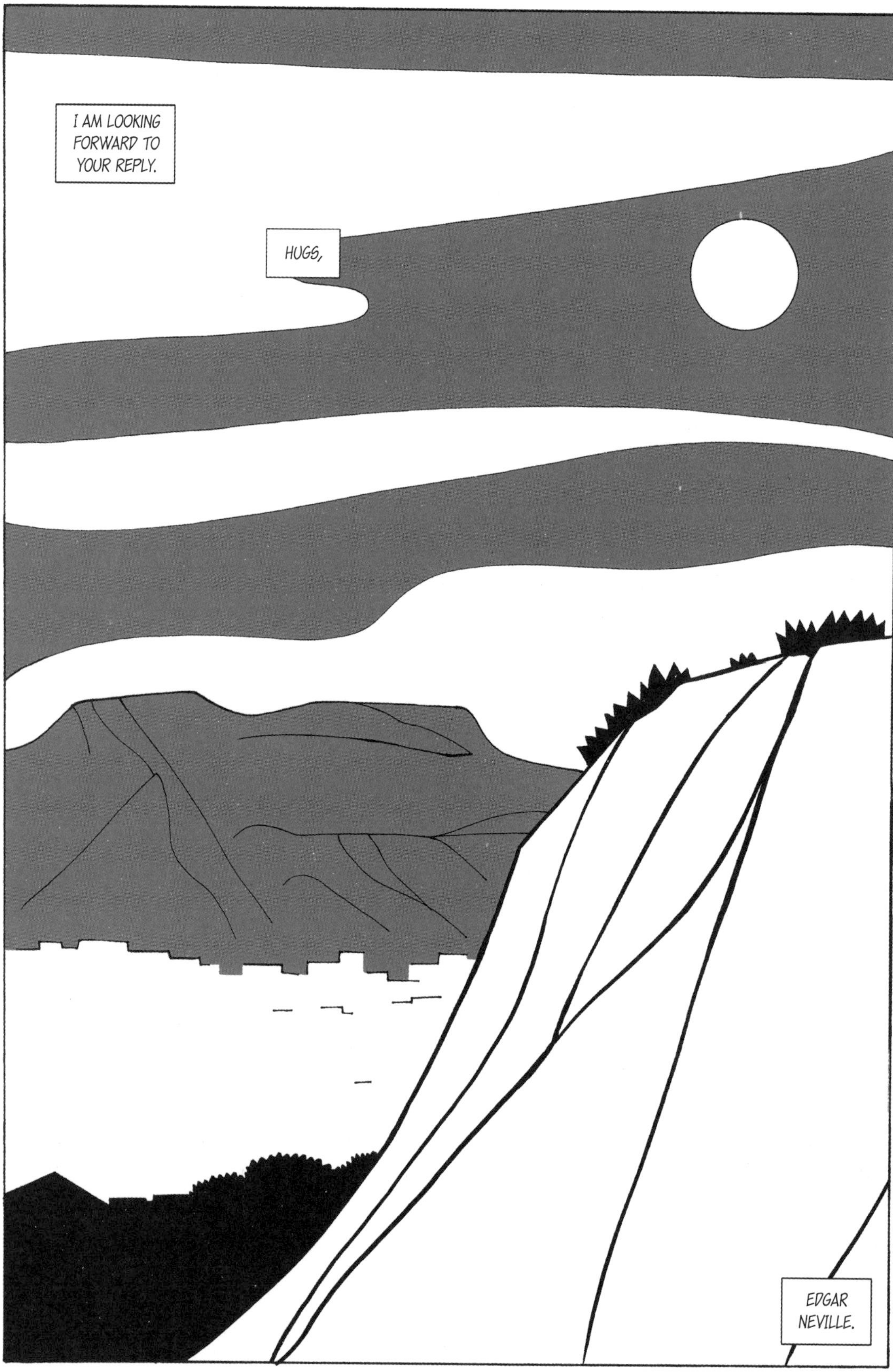
I AM LOOKING FORWARD TO YOUR REPLY.
HUGS,
EDGAR NEVILLE.

Spaniards in Movieland

Estrella de Diego

PROFESSOR OF ART HISTORY, COMPLUTENSE UNIVERSITY OF MADRID

Sometimes the life we find ends up being the life we want. That is what happens to a certain traveler keen on moving, when he arrives at LAX, Los Angeles International Airport. Amid the hustle and bustle and the smell of gasoline, open spaces are advertised insistently, a prelude to unexpected situations. Welcome to California.

From there, we travel by car along the highways, at once crowded and sluggish, leading to the metropolis, with so many city centers, so scattered, like a supersized Sophronia. And just like Calvino's "invisible city," Los Angeles is made up of two half-cities — one permanent and the other temporary. The first half, the circus-city, is, paradoxically, the stable one, the one that stays, the one that does not pack up its things and leave. This is the last fabricated town center where the Broad Museum, the opera building and the cathedral of Moneo are located: it is *Downtown LA*. The second half-city, "with the bank, the factories, the palaces, the slaughterhouse, the school and everything else," is dismantled when the season is over. The conditional becomes permanent. That which is settled, movable.

That moving half is a juggling act with quite a lot of movie props and floating letters that, from a distance, seem to be stuck to the mountain. In this center of centers, one of the first neighborhoods to define what this city represents for the world, a city in flux, where everything is for sale and everything is temporary, the most spectacular staging unfolds. Welcome to Hollywood.

There, the bold traveler — guided by a local who prefers not to use the highways to travel through the city — ventures out to walk along the long avenue that crosses the map. And he can see how Hollywood Boulevard is actually full of a colorful mix of people — it is not true that everyone travels by car in Los Angeles. Perhaps, he will choose to have dinner at Musso & Frank Grill — a classic spot that opened in 1919, when the silent film era was still in full swing. When he goes in, he is overwhelmed by the memories of everything he has witnessed on the screen, and the ghosts come without being summoned.

A handsome man with gel-coated hair has just escaped from the silver screen and his distinguished look evokes the glitz and glitter of yesteryear. Top hat, tuxedo, white scarf... for a moment the look on his face resembles the way stars used to look long ago in Hollywood, when movies were silent; he makes us lose our heads, just as moviegoers reacted to the debut of Greta Garbo. This sexy woman and the attractive man starred together in one of the diva's first films, *The Temptress* (1926); after Metro paired her with Antonio Moreno in the film, she went on to become the most famous vamp in the history of cinema.

A while ago, on the Walk of Fame, his name on the ground either went unnoticed or was mistaken for that of a Mexican star. In spite of everything, Antonio Moreno — known as Tony Moreno to some — was the first Spaniard to achieve success in that Movieland to which Ramón Gómez de la Serna dedicated a book in 1923; the '20s, when an entire generation became fascinated by everything that happens without *really* happening — the magic of cinema.

In *Movieland,* Ramón describes the glorious years of silent movies — still a thriving genre when the book was published — when the eyes alone were responsible for telling the story. "For cinematographers, the voice, the word, the nuanced and elegant diction is in their eyes. They became 'cinematographically mute,' one might say," he writes, referring to the retinal damage film stars suffered under the bright lights.

However, the powerful spotlights were not the only thing that put an end to the intense gaze of silent film actors. After the arrival of the first "talkies," some of the brightest stars stopped shining. The old stars and their exaggerated gestures were unable to adapt to the new demands of the script, as the film *Singing in the Rain* portrays in such a funny and eloquent manner. Antonio Moreno was one of those victims, his California stardom extinguished by the rise of the other great Latin lover whose fame eclipsed all others: Rodolfo (Rudolph) Valentino, whose film career was kicked off with the 1921 film *The Four Horsemen of the Apocalypse* (scripted by a fellow Spaniard, Blasco Ibañez). As is often the case in Hollywood, Valentino's untimely death played in his favor, cementing his status as a cinema icon. Moreno would later become a famous director in Mexico, but that is another story.

Antonio Moreno was not, in any case, the only Spaniard to triumph in the so-called "Mecca of the Movies." A few extraordinary characters — at times unnoticed — found the life they ended up wanting in Hollywood, even if it was not exactly what they had been searching for. This was the case for Edgar Neville, the most extravagant character of the Spanish avant-garde. He was a career diplomat, adventurous and curious; his political positions fluctuated; his tastes were exquisite and extravagant; in short, he was a true *bon vivant*, described by Ramón as "raised on elephant's milk brought from India." He was close to the Málaga poets of *Sur* magazine, a friendship that was cut short by the Spanish Civil War. Neville landed at the Washington, D.C. Embassy in 1928 and traveled to Hollywood on his first holiday. For that reason and that reason alone, he had decided to accept the post. Hollywood would be his primary destination for at least the next four years.

Bearing a title of nobility, the Count of Berlanga del Duero, Edgar Neville made a grand entrance when he arrived in California. His aristocratic roots and demeanor afforded him with letters of introduction from Grace Vanderbilt and other important families on the east coast. He soon became a fixture in Hollywood, and had a crucial role in finding work for his compatriots in the film industry. From 1930 onwards, other Spaniards arrived under his guidance and started to settle in Hollywood, partly attracted by the talkies, which necessitated dubbing into other languages in order to enter into foreign markets. And at a time when the major studios were organizing departments to produce versions of their films in various languages, Neville supervised the Spanish Department of Metro-Goldwyn-Mayer. Jardiel Poncela, Tono de Lara and José López Rubio found their place there and even Buñuel himself was lured to Hollywood by Metro — although he stayed less than a year, and spent most of that time at Charlie Chaplin's house, where many Spaniards in the cinema world congregated. This Spanish contingent became so numerous that Scott Fitzgerald called Chaplin's house in Beverly Hills "The House of Spain," because it was open to all Spaniards in the city. Neville and Chaplin became close friends, of course.

Around that time, another Spaniard met with success in Movieland, in front of the camera — Conchita Montenegro. She paved the way for the bevy of Spanish beauties who would join her later in the 1950s, such as Sarita Montiel and Carmen Sevilla, who — as she herself said — took to her heels from the studio tired of the gentlemen who could not keep their hands to themselves. Conchita Montenegro, with her seductive, smiling eyes, even went so far as to make real "American" films, in English, after painstaking preparation. In 1931, she shot a love story with a touch of exotic beauty: *Never the Twain Shall Meet* by W.S. Van Dyke. One of the main actors, Leslie Howard — who would later star in *Gone with the Wind* (1939) — was to become the actress's great love. Legend has it that Howard was also a secret agent for Britain, and in 1943 embarked on a mission to negotiate Franco's neutrality at Churchill's request. Reality always surpasses fiction: on his way back to London his plane was shot down by Luftwaffe fighters, leaving Montenegro so distraught that she decided to walk away from the screen.

However, the succession of great Spanish beauties in Hollywood had just begun. In fact, it has continued with Penelope Cruz, just as Banderas and Bardem are the successors to Moreno and Valentino. It often seems that Spanish actors in Hollywood play themselves, without completely breaking the spell: desirable and passionate Latinos. Sara Montiel stood up against this ethnic typecasting so typical of the star system. In the 1950s, she captivated a Hollywood that was thirsty for sex symbols and fought against the "Hispanic" role with which she was typecast. For this reason, she refused an exclusive contract worth millions with one of the major studios and even went so far as to play an "Indian" role — portraying a Native American, braids and all. Of course, unlike many other Spaniards in Hollywood, Montiel never lost her head when she arrived in Sophronia. Like Madonna in the '80s, she was in control of her career as a sex symbol until after her wedding to her first husband, director Anthony Mann. Perhaps Montiel always did whatever she wanted.

A few years earlier, Valencian pianist José Iturbi — brother of the pianist Amparo Iturbi, who also made a career in Hollywood — had arrived in California. After playing the piano here and there, Iturbi was hired by Metro, and went on to perform in such popular sequences as the one in *Anchors Aweigh* (dir. George Sidney, 1945), the famous musical starring Gene Kelly and Frank Sinatra. In this well-known scene, he plays Franz Liszt's Hungarian Rhapsody No. 2 in what appears to be a multiple-piano recital where boys and girls show their dexterity with the octaves. From a contemporary perspective, Iturbi, a professional pianist, also exploited his racialized role. In a 1940 interview in *The Evening Star*, he does not talk about Schubert or even Granados — instead, he talks about Spanish food, which "Americans often think is similar to Mexican food, although it is very different." A curious way of relying on the "exoticism" of his country of origin when describing *paella* or the Spanish potato omelette, *tortilla de patatas*. Spanish or Mexican, it made no difference: it was all "Latin food."

Another luminary among Spaniards in Hollywood was Xavier Cugat, whose family emigrated to Cuba when he was three years old. He was a *bon vivant*, a caricaturist and musician. His life was a hustle; he tried his hand at rhumba, breeding Chihuahuas, hawking products at the entrance of cinemas. Throughout his career, he made many connections in Hollywood: friendships with actors Mae West, Lana Turner, Rita Hayworth and Carmen Miranda, with whom he starred in many successful films, and *partnerships* with explosive women, from Abbe Lane to Charo Baeza, a Murcian who, little known in Spain even today, has triumphed in the United States while playing up her "exotic" qualities, such as her strongly accented English.

But it was not only writers and actors and actresses who took their dreams to *Movieland*. One of the most famous Spaniards in Hollywood was Salvador Dalí, especially notable for his collaboration with Alfred Hitchcock on the 1945 film *Spellbound*, starring Ingrid Bergman and Gregory Peck. The scene that portrays the reconstruction of memory — or rather of what has been forgotten — is one of the most remarkable sequences in the history of cinema for its spectacular staging and psychoanalytical precision, which Dalí knew better than anyone else. In this particular case, however, Hollywood's movie magic could not measure up to Dalí's dreams: in the eyes of the surrealist painter, Movieland was a prudish place, especially when Hitchcock had to explain to him — as the director recalled years later in an interview — that Hollywood had its rules,

and he could not pour live ants all over Ingrid Bergman.

The times of *Un Chien Andalou* (*An Andalusian Dog*), the collaboration between Dalí and Buñuel in 1929, had passed. In Hollywood, almost 30 years later, things were done differently, perhaps because Hollywood — the stable half of Sophronia — was, at least in 1945 (and even today, despite appearances), a harmless place in hectic LA. "Hollywood is a lovely place. Without a doubt, one of the nicest and most welcoming places in the world. It deserves nothing but praise," said Edgar Neville in an interview with Florentino Hernández Girbal for *Cinegramas* in June 1935.

And as we make our way towards downtown, the sign seems to slowly fade away into the mountainside. Then Hollywood, the stable city, gives way to the other half, the one that is dismantled every season to be reborn. Welcome to Los Angeles.

ART

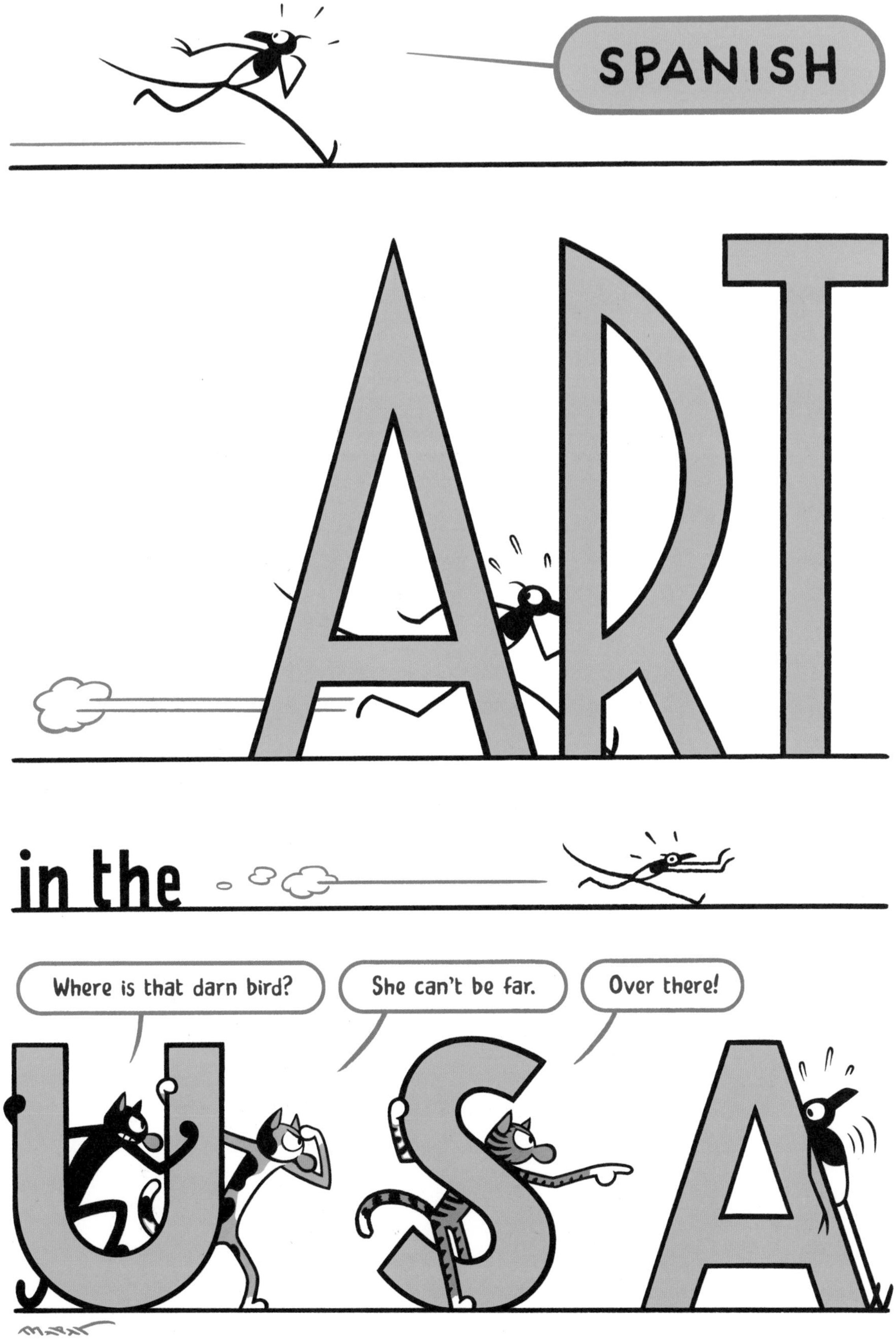
SPANISH
ART
in the
Where is that darn bird?
She can't be far.
Over there!
USA

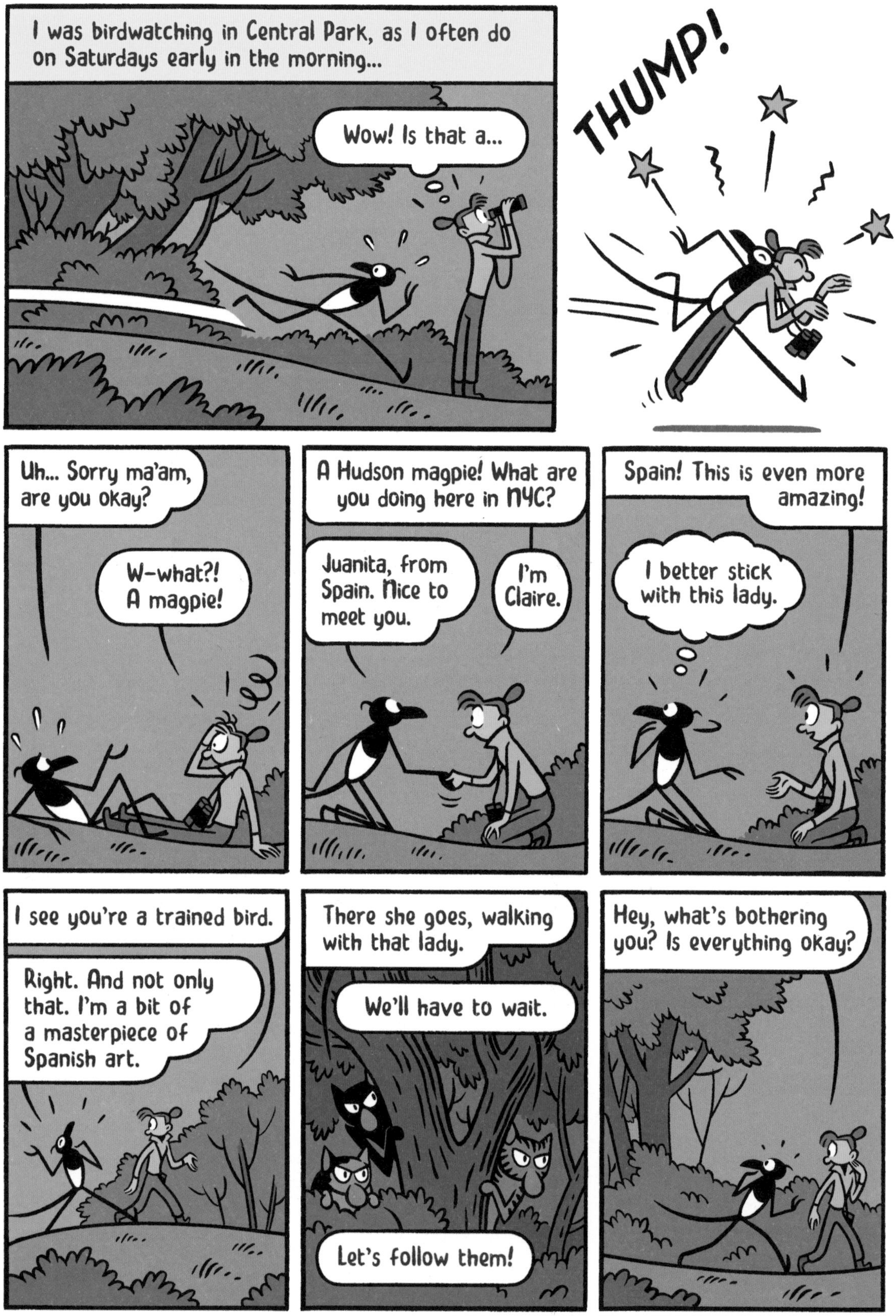
I was birdwatching in Central Park, as I often do on Saturdays early in the morning...
Wow! Is that a...
THUMP!
Uh... Sorry ma'am, are you okay?
W-what?! A magpie!
A Hudson magpie! What are you doing here in NYC?
Juanita, from Spain. Nice to meet you.
I'm Claire.
Spain! This is even more amazing!
I better stick with this lady.
I see you're a trained bird.
Right. And not only that. I'm a bit of a masterpiece of Spanish art.
There she goes, walking with that lady.
We'll have to wait.
Let's follow them!
Hey, what's bothering you? Is everything okay?

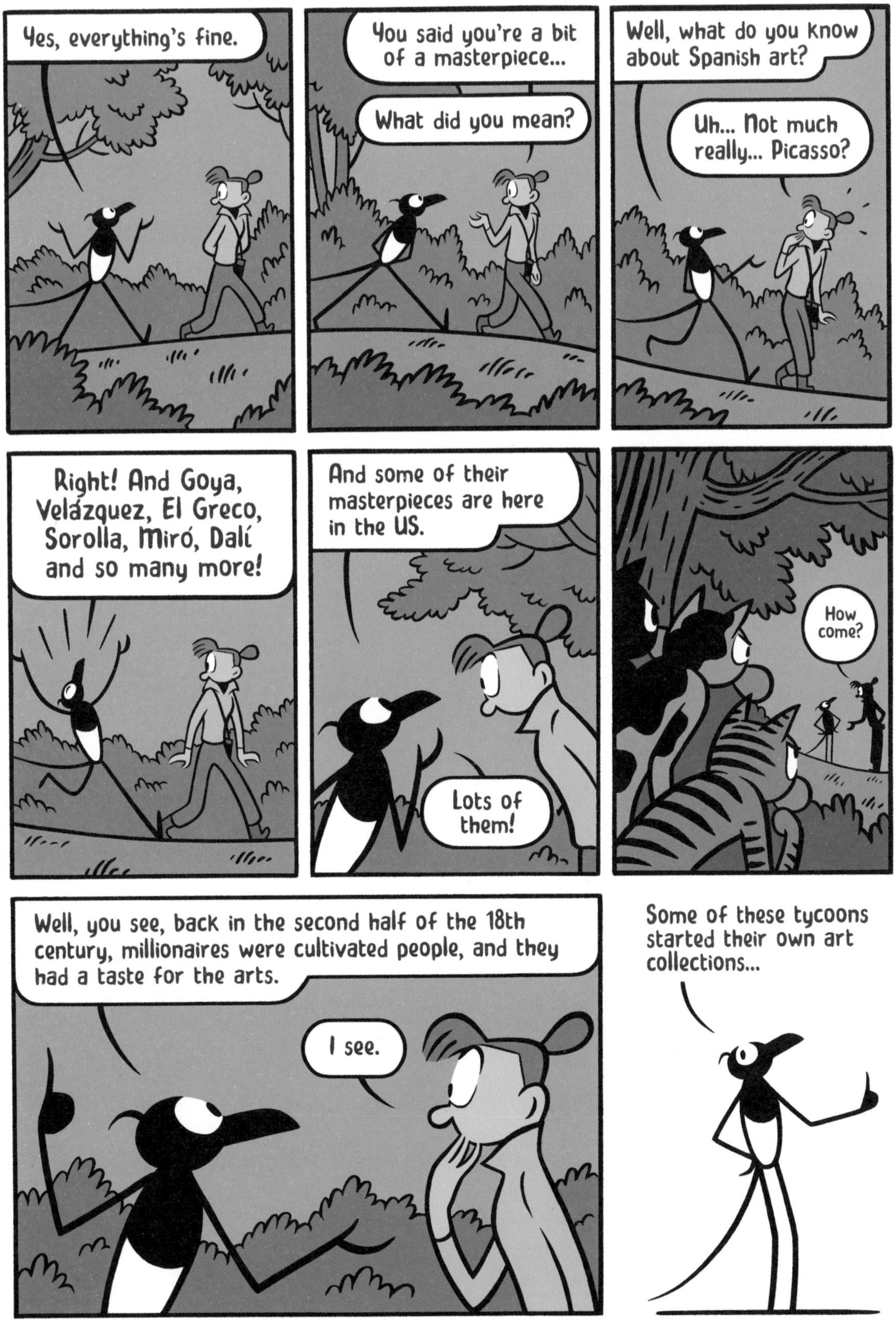
Yes, everything's fine.
You said you're a bit of a masterpiece...
What did you mean?
Well, what do you know about Spanish art?
Uh... Not much really... Picasso?
Right! And Goya, Velázquez, El Greco, Sorolla, Miró, Dalí and so many more!
And some of their masterpieces are here in the US.
Lots of them!
How come?
Well, you see, back in the second half of the 18th century, millionaires were cultivated people, and they had a taste for the arts.
I see.
Some of these tycoons started their own art collections...

They travelled to Europe and acquired art and antiques there.

Italian paintings from the 17th century were considered to be the finest and most refined paintings, but Spanish art was also very much appreciated because it was regarded as... hmm... somewhat eccentric.

I'll take it. My secretary will handle all the details.

At the time, there was this romantic image of Spain as an enigmatic and exotic land, full of ancient ruins from a decadent past.

The US collected all kinds of treasures from Spain's past. Whole medieval cloisters were bought and shipped here, stone by stone.

In 1904, Archer Milton Huntington founded the Hispanic Society of America in New York City...

...which was devoted to the study, promotion and preservation of Spanish art.

Other famous collectors of art from Spain were Henry C. Frick, Louisine and Henry Havemeyer, William Randolph Hearst, David Rockefeller...

Henry Clay Frick

Archer Milton Huntington

Louisine & Henry Havemeyer

David Rockefeller

After the First World War, museums were created, mostly thanks to the donations and contributions made by these philanthropists.

The MoMA (Museum of Modern Art) opened in 1929 and was absolutely instrumental in establishing Picasso as the great master of 20th century art thanks to a huge exhibition of his works in 1940.

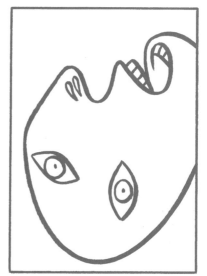

"Guernica", probably his most famous painting, was entrusted by the artist to the MoMA. It remained on display from 1939 until 1981, when it was returned to Spain after regaining democracy, as per Picasso's wishes.

Many American intellectuals and artists were greatly influenced by Spanish art, particularly abstract expressionist painters who, in turn, had a great impact on Spanish abstract art later.

During the last decades of the 20th century, numerous Spanish artists moved to the US in search of success.

The interest for Spanish art has grown significantly and as a result, nowadays there are thousands of Spanish masterpieces on view in museums, other institutions and even in public areas all across the US.

Crown Fountain by Jaume Plensa, Millennium Park, Chicago

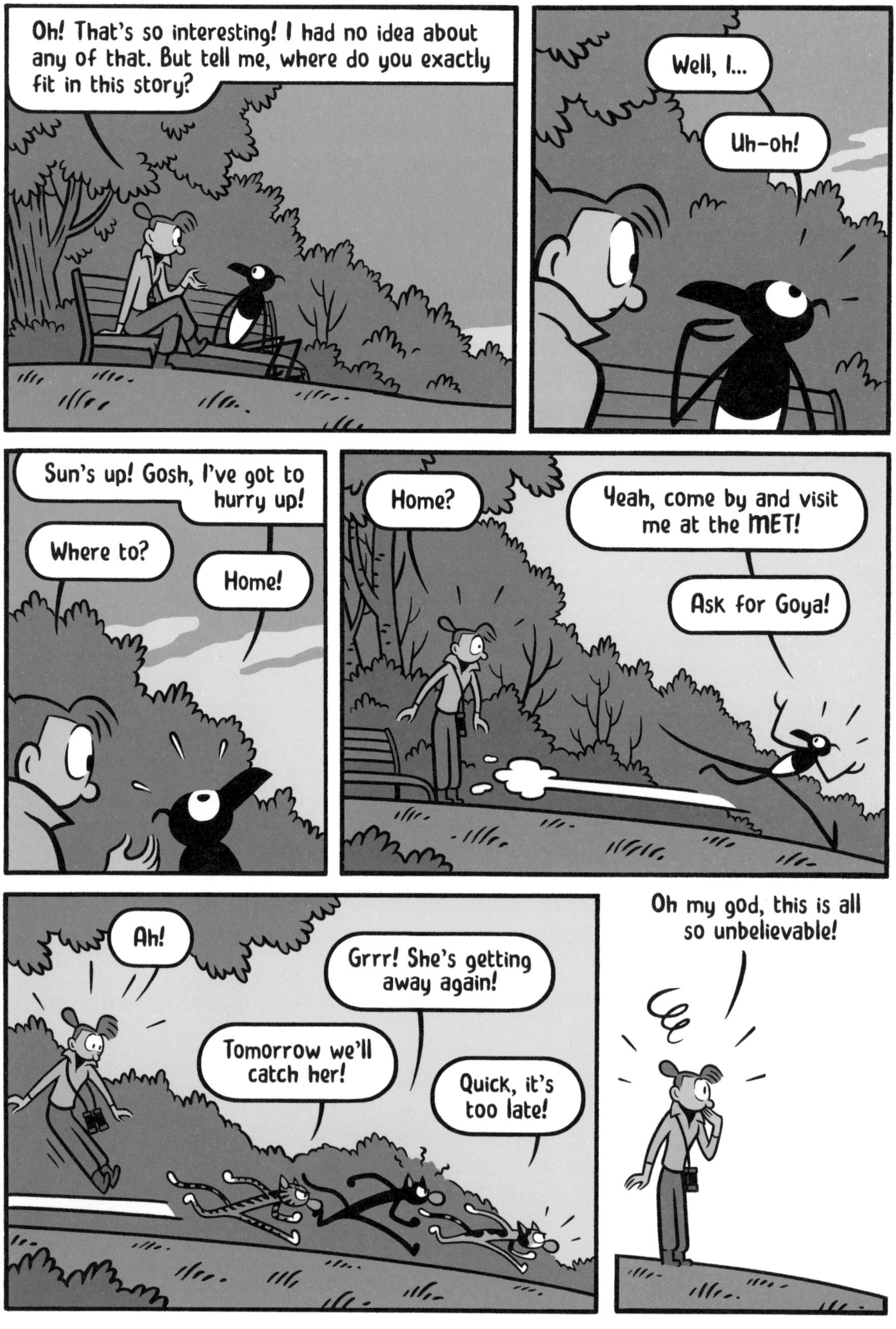
Oh! That's so interesting! I had no idea about any of that. But tell me, where do you exactly fit in this story?
Well, I...
Uh-oh!
Sun's up! Gosh, I've got to hurry up!
Where to?
Home!
Home?
Yeah, come by and visit me at the MET!
Ask for Goya!
Ah!
Grrr! She's getting away again!
Tomorrow we'll catch her!
Quick, it's too late!
Oh my god, this is all so unbelievable!

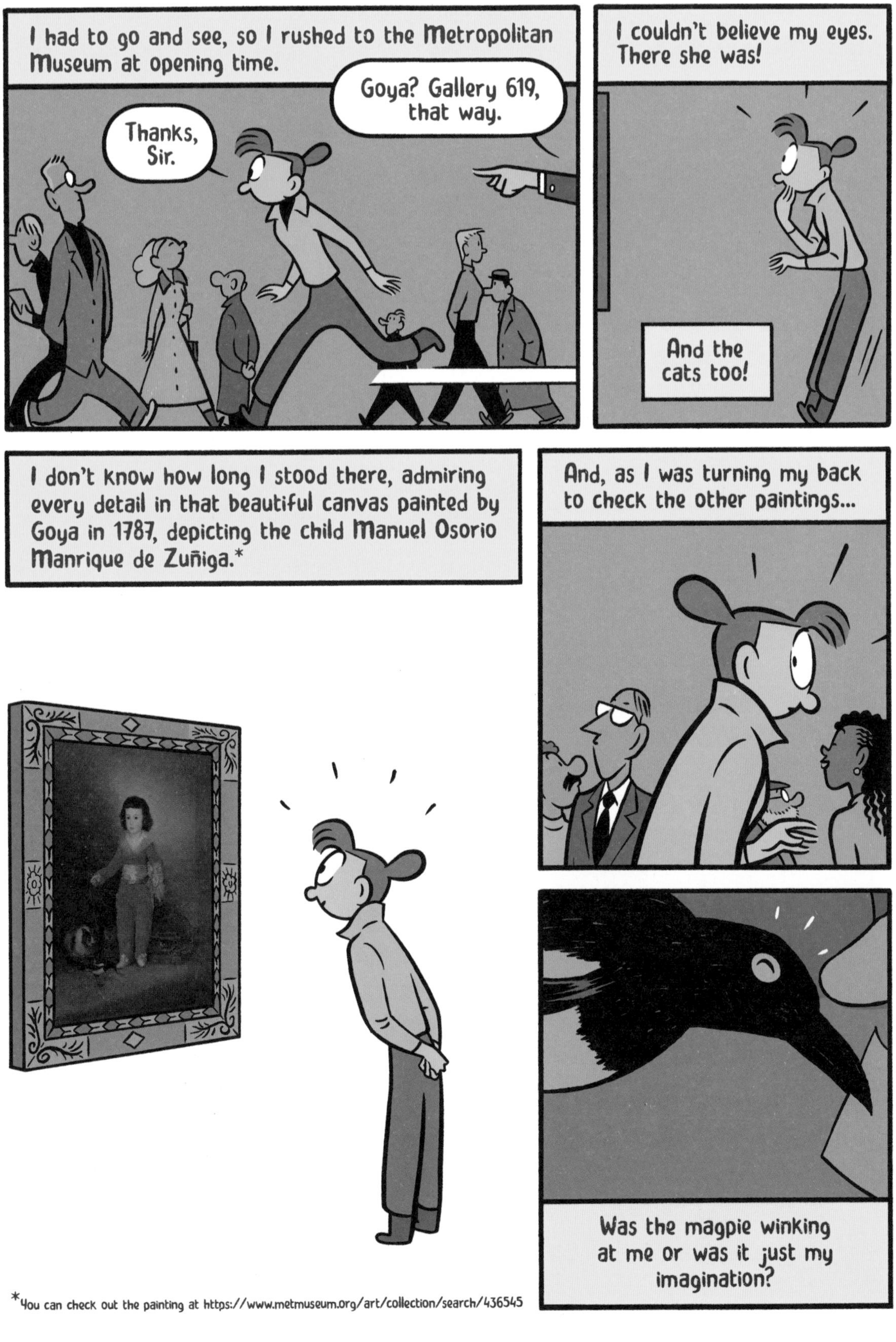
I had to go and see, so I rushed to the Metropolitan Museum at opening time.
Goya? Gallery 619, that way.
Thanks, Sir.
I couldn't believe my eyes. There she was!
And the cats too!
I don't know how long I stood there, admiring every detail in that beautiful canvas painted by Goya in 1787, depicting the child Manuel Osorio Manrique de Zuñiga.*
And, as I was turning my back to check the other paintings...
Was the magpie winking at me or was it just my imagination?

*You can check out the painting at https://www.metmuseum.org/art/collection/search/436545

Spanish Art in the United States

María Dolores Jiménez-Blanco

PROFESSOR OF ART HISTORY, COMPLUTENSE UNIVERSITY OF MADRID

INITIALLY, SPANISH ART started being collected by North Americans as a private initiative, which was later followed by museums. It also had a privileged setting, New York City, where many of the largest collections were housed and where some of the most important American artists worked, such as Pollock, Motherwell and Gorky, who expressed their fascination with Spanish art and culture. This fascination was reflected in the Hispanic Society of America, which became its emblem. Created by Archer Milton Huntington in 1904, this institution focused on the conservation, study and social promotion of Spain's historical and artistic legacy. This project was part of a new wave of taste for all things Spanish that grew well beyond the limits of art collecting and academic scholarship to reach the most varied aspects of everyday American life. In the first decades of the 20th century, it could be said that everything related to Spain came into vogue, influenced by Hollywood movies which contributed to its trendiness — or trivialization. A token of this Spanish trend can be found in certain styles of architecture or interior design that appeared in the South and West of the United States dubbed the "Spanish Style," reaching one of its peaks in California around 1915 with the Panama California Exposition.

The initial interest in Spanish art from the Golden Age was later extended to more recent time periods. During this process, Spanish art shifted from being perceived as an eccentric footnote in the history of art to being placed at the very center of the canon within the context of modernity. In the wake of the so-called "romantic image of Spain," to which American writers such as Washington Irving had also contributed during the last third of the 19th century, an interest in Spanish art was consolidated for being an exotic model — that is to say, external to the Western canon.

Between 1860 and 1920, Spanish culture was being discovered at the same time that the Spanish empire was beginning its decline and the US was rising to the status of a major world power. The year 1898 dramatically marked this period with the Spanish-American War that ended Spanish colonial rule in the Americas. Obtaining Spain's cultural treasures was a symbolic way for the new American empire to assert its supremacy over the old Spanish empire. Spain then was regarded as a mysterious and decadent country, full of Christian, Arab and Jewish ruins, proud of its past dominance in Spanish America, picturesque in its backwardness and customs and very attractive for its history — a dark image that somehow survived in the Hispanic Society, albeit coexisting with the regenerative vision of the *Institución Libre de Enseñanza* (Free Institution of Education).

Among the first collections in the United States to include Spanish paintings was that of Joseph Bonaparte, Napoleon's brother, who, after becoming King of Spain, settled in Bordentown, New Jersey, in 1815, and kept several works by Velázquez and Murillo in his residence. The love for collecting would later spark an interest among a group of wealthy Americans who emerged with the rapid economic development of the Gilded Age. Eager to emulate the customs of the European aristocracy, they acquired pieces on a large scale, placing particular emphasis on Spanish art.

The outbreak of the First World War put an end to the treasure hunting taking place in Europe by the Morgans, Hearst, Frick and Havemeyer. Those great collectors would soon give way to museums. Collecting shifted from being based on passion and a desire to project a social image to institutional collecting meant to be systematic and for educational purposes. The interwar period would be a crucial time for great American museums in general, and New York would see the consolidation of the Metropolitan Museum of Art (The Met) and the founding of the Museum of Modern Art (MoMA).

The Met managed to bring together very important collections that included Spanish art. For example, John D. Rockefeller, Jr. contributed the spectacular museum of medieval Christian art known as The Cloisters, in Tryon Park. The periods of Spanish art best represented were medieval Christian paintings, Hispanic-Muslim decorative arts, the Golden Age and the 20th-century Vanguards. Additionally, there is the *Patio from the Castle of Vélez Blanco* — an architectural marvel from the Renaissance that formerly belonged to George Blumenthal — and the famous grille from the Cathedral of Valladolid, donated by W.R. Hearst in 1956.

In the Met's collection of 15th- to 19th-century European paintings (along with some works by Zurbarán and Ribera and Spanish altarpieces from the 15th century) the canvases of three great artists of the so-called "Spanish School" stand out: El Greco, Velázquez and Goya. From El Greco (and the legacy of Henry and Louisine Havemeyer), we find *The View of Toledo* and the *Portrait of the Cardinal*, as well as the religious canvas of *The Vision of Saint John*. The relationship between this work and Picasso's *Les Demoiselles d'Avignon*, now in the MoMA, is clearly evident. Picasso was introduced to this painting by El Greco in the studio of painter Ignacio Zuloaga in Paris. Of all the Spanish artworks in the Met, the portrait of *Juan de Pareja* by Diego de Silva y Velázquez is perhaps the best known. In 1970, the Met bought the portrait of *Juan de Pareja* at auction for the then-record price of $5,592,000. The portrait of the boy, *Don Manuel Osorio Manrique de Zúñiga*, is Francisco de Goya's most emblematic work. There, we can also find drawings and engravings by Goya such as the first editions of the complete albums of *Los Caprichos* (The Whims), *Los Desastres de la Guerra* (The Disasters of War), *La Tauromaquia* (Bullfighting) and the aquatint *The Giant*.

The first Picasso entered the Met's collection in 1946, a portrait of the writer and collector Gertrude Stein, and in 1949 the personal collection of photographer and gallery owner Alfred

Stiegliz — which included nine Picassos dating between 1901 and 1912 — was incorporated into the museum. An additional 80 pieces of Cubist art — including collages, drawings, paintings and sculptures by Picasso, Juan Gris, Braque and Leger — was donated by Leonard Lauder. Joan Miró also gained presence thanks to donations from Pierre and Gaetana Matisse, who also contributed works by Millares, Rivera and Saura. Dalí is also present with the canvas *The Lace Maker, After Vermeer* from the Lehman Collection.

The Department of Photography has images by Ortiz Echagüe, and the Musical Instruments Department has a guitar by Andrés Segovia, made by Manuel Ramírez in 1912. The Costume Institute keeps a caftan designed by Mariano Fortuny de Madrazo around 1920 and a ball gown from the 1948 spring–summer season by Basque fashion designer Cristóbal Balenciaga.

The MoMA, created in 1929, shaped contemporary aesthetics and developed the definition of modern art. The presence of Spanish artists such as Picasso, Miró, Dalí, Juan Gris and Julio González is of particular importance as they are considered to be the pillars of international modernity. Picasso's *Guernica*, which was exhibited at MoMA until 1981, and *Les Demoiselles d'Avignon* are, in this sense, crucial. But its collections include the work of many other artists from later generations, such as Tàpies and Saura, representative of the new Spanish avant-garde after the Spanish Civil War. They were part of the same generation as the artists of the New York School, the school that marked "the triumph of American painting," and thanks to which New York City supplanted Paris as the world's art capital. There, we can also find works by recent artists such as Sicilia, Barceló and Juan Muñoz, photographers such as Joan Fontcuberta, architects from Gaudí to Bofill and filmmakers such as Almodóvar.

In 1960, the Solomon R. Guggenheim Museum, also in New York, devoted its first exhibition in Frank Lloyd Wright's building to Spanish art, entitled: *Before Picasso, after Miró*. In 1982, another exhibition was organized, *New Images from Spain*, which reflected the post-Franco art scene. Later, in 2007, the museum held an exhibition entitled: *Spanish Painting from El Greco to Picasso: Time, Truth and History*. Once again, Picasso is the Spanish artist best represented in the Guggenheim collection (with more than 50 pieces, half of them from the Tanhauser collection), followed by Miró, Gris and Tàpies. But it is worth remembering that the Guggenheim also houses works from later generations of Spanish artists, such as Chillida and Guerrero, which showcase the vital connection between Spanish art and American abstract expressionism.

There are exhibitions of Spanish art in other — perhaps less intuitive — museums, such as the Jewish Museum (bibles), the Whitney Museum (José de Creeft, Esteban Vicente) and the Brooklyn Museum (Zuloaga). But Spanish presence is not strictly limited to New York. The National Gallery of Washington has magnificent collections thanks to philanthropists such as Andrew W. Mellon, Chester Dale — whose patronage activities were particularly important in the field of contemporary art (particularly Picasso's *The Family of Saltimbanques*, 1905; Salvador Dalí's *The Last Supper*, 1955, commissioned expressly by Dale, and five paintings by Zuloaga) — and Samuel H. Kress (who acquired El Greco's *Laocconte and His Sons* for this museum). One of the most striking pieces is Murillo's *Two Women at the Window*, acquired during the Second World War as a gift from the Widener family. Another piece, Miró's *The Farm*, which belonged to Hemingway, was also added later. But Velázquez's *The Seamstress*, a donation made by Andrew Mellon in 1937, stands out from the others. It is also interesting to note that the NGA's 50th anniversary was celebrated with the acquisition of José de Ribera's painting *Martyrdom of Saint Bartholomew* for five million dollars.

From coast to coast, other institutions also house important Spanish pieces. For example, at the Museum of Fine Arts in Boston, two monumental heads by Antonio López, *Night & Day*, welcome visitors, who once inside will find frescoes from a 12th-century Catalan chapel. Not far away, the Isabella Stewart Gardner Museum has a so-called Spanish Room which exhibits *El Jaleo*, the most Spanish-style painting by the American painter John Singer Sargent.

The Philadelphia Museum of Fine Arts contains altarpieces by Bernat Martorell, Zurbarán and Goya, the other version of Picasso's canvas *The Three Musicians* (1921), Miró's *Dog Barking at the Moon* (1926) — one of Miró's best-known pieces in America — as well as a striking piece by Dalí: *Soft Construction with Boiled Beans (Premonition of Civil War)* (1936), from the prestigious Louise and Walter Arensberg Collection. In St. Petersburg, Florida, an entire museum is dedicated to Dalí, which originated from the private collection of Eleanor and Reynolds Morse, who met Dalí personally at an exhibition devoted to him at MoMA in 1941.

The Art Institute of Chicago holds part of the collection of the American tycoon Charles Deering, which includes some medieval altarpieces. But perhaps its greatest Spanish treasure is El Greco's *Assumption of the Virgin*, acquired by the museum from art dealer Durand Ruel in 1906. The Art Institute was also the first American museum to exhibit the work of Picasso, right after the Armory Show in 1913, which was also held there.

The San Diego Museum of Art, whose building is a true manifesto of adherence to California's Spanish heritage inside the Balboa Park complex, has a facade inspired by the University of Salamanca, but its sculptures depict Velázquez, Ribera and Murillo, with busts of Ribera and El Greco. With more than 300 Spanish works, it presents the history of Spanish painting from the 15th to the 20th century. In fact, the number one piece in the museum's inventory is Sorolla's *María at La Granja*, donated by Archer Milton Huntington. Similarly related to the university environment, the Meadows Museum in Dallas, at SMU, is another institution devoted to Spanish culture. Inaugurated in 1965, it holds a collection assembled by the oil tycoon and art collector Algur H. Meadows. Meadows was committed to the search for oil in Spain, which is why from 1950 onwards he travelled frequently to Spain; staying at the Ritz Hotel in Madrid, he often visited the neighboring Prado Museum, which led him to acquire Spanish art. In 1961, he donated his collection of 75 paintings along with a million dollars to build the museum. During the following decade, the collection was consolidated, and today the institution has set a standard with a diverse collection of more than 300 pieces, ranging from the *San Sebastian* by Yáñez de la Almedina to the *Femme Asisse* by María Blanchard.

Since the 19th century, Spanish art has been a constant presence in the US from coast to coast. While the interest may have initially centered on the antinormative side of Spanish tradition, external to the canon — particularly work from the Golden Age — Spanish art ended up finding its place in the history of Western art, normalizing its presence and becoming a key element in the context of the avant-garde, whose canon is constructed precisely against the academic norm.

BIOGRAPHIES

Cartoonists
Scholars

Sonia Pulido (b. 1973, Barcelona) lives and works in a seaside village near Barcelona. She contributes illustrations to various newspapers and magazines including *The New Yorker*, *The New York Times*, *Columbia Journalism Review*, *Propublica*, *The Wall Street Journal*, *AD France*, *El País Semanal*, *The Boston Globe*, *Harper's Baazar Spain*, *Rockdelux*, *Marie Claire*, *Variety*, *La maleta de Portbou*, *Jot Down* and *Orsai*, among others. She also creates covers and illustrations for numerous book projects, including *Mujeres bacanas Latinas*, *Montserrat Roig Tots els contes* and *El mejor de los pecados*. Her original graphic novel is *La Madeja* (2014).

Lola Moral Ruz (b. 1964, Montalbán) studied Fine Arts at the University of Granada. She has worked as a scriptwriter and colorist for the publishing houses Toon Books (USA), Dargaud, Delcourt, Dupuis, Actes Sud (France), Ediciones Santillana and Dibbuks (Spain). She has collaborated with Sergio García on several books, including *Los 3 Caminos*, *Dexter London* and *Mono*

& Lobo. In addition to her work in the publishing industry, she makes a variety of sculptures and textile creations.

Sergio García Sánchez (b. 1967, Guadix) studied Fine Arts at the University of Granada. He teaches at the University of Granada, was a guest teacher at the Master Bd EESI Angoulême and frequently runs other workshops and lectures. He specializes in comics, editorial illustration and children's illustration, and his clients include *The New York Times*, *The New Yorker*, *El País Semanal*, *El País Babelia*, Toon Books, Dargaud, Delcourt, Dibbuks, Ediciones Santillana and Ediciones SM, among others. His work has been recognized by Premios ÑH (2019–2020), FESPA (2020), APIM (2019), The Society of Illustrators (2016), *American Illustration* (AI37), *School Library Journal* (2016), *Kirkus* (2016), Festival Internacional de Bande Dessinnée de Sierre (2001) and CBBD-Centre Belge de la Bande Déssinne.

Rayco Pulido Rodríguez (b. 1978, Telde, Gran Canaria) is a cartoonist and teacher. In addition to his illustration work for outlets such as *El País*, he is the author of six graphic novels. His 2016 comic *Lamia* won a residency grant from Acción Cultural Española (ACE) and *La Maison*

des Auteurs (Angoulême, France), as well as Spain's National Comics Award in 2017. His other works include *Final Feliz* (with Hernán Migoya, 2004), *Sordo* (with David Muñoz, 2008), *Sin Título, 2008–2011* (2011) and *Nela* (2013). His work has been published in Spain, France and the United States.

Ana Penyas (b. 1987, Valencia) has a degree in Fine Arts from the Polytechnic University of Valencia. In 2017, she was awarded the Fnac-Salamandra Graphic Novel Award, which led her to publish her first graphic novel, *Estamos todas bien*. In 2018, she won the Best New Talent Award at the Barcelona International Comics Fair and Spain's National Comics Award for her work *Estamos todas bien*. She has also illustrated several books, often centered around historical memory, including *En transición* and *Mexique, el nombre del barco*. Her second graphic novel, *Todo bajo el sol*, was published in 2021.

Seisdedos (b. 1979, Lorca) is the alter ego of Álvaro García. Growing up in Granada, he earned a degree in history and explored various career paths before pursuing illustration full time. His work lies at the crossroads of social criticism, surrealism and pop culture. Since 2006, he has provided illustrations and articles to such media outlets as *Grenada Today*, *Negratinta* and *CTXT*. He has written and/or illustrated many books, including *La Alhambra* (2016), *El ruiseñor sin ojos: 52 cantes ilustrados* (2017) and *1922, una mirada al pasado* (2019). His art has appeared in exhibitions across Spain, in Cádiz, Seville and Grenada.

Anapurna (b. 1990, Palma) is the alter ego of Ana Sainz Quesada. Based in Madrid, she is a graduate in Fine Arts from the University of Barcelona and specialized in illustration and graphic narrative from IED Madrid. She works in a variety of artistic disciplines including drawing, painting, street art, embroidery and engraving, but she loves making and reading comics above all. Her first graphic novel, *Chucrut*, was published in 2015 and won the Fnac-Salamandra Graphic Novel Award. Her work has been featured in various magazines around the world, including *Larva* (Colombia), *Kiblind Magazine* (France) and *Jot Down* (Spain), and included in graphic anthologies in the United States (Anthology Editions) and Germany (Wagenbach).

Carla Berrocal (b. 1983, Madrid) studied illustration and graphic design in Madrid. In 2004, her cartooning career kicked off with her pulp-themed work *Hire, el terrible vampiro samurai*, written by Daniel Hartwell. Her first solo graphic novel, *El Brujo*, was published in 2011. Her work has been featured in various publications, including *Hundlebert Syndrome*, *Revista Fierro*, *Quimera*, *Monográfico* and *Nobrow*. In 2019, she obtained an artist residency at the Royal Spanish Academy in Rome, where she completed her comic project *Doña Concha* (Reservoir Books), which chronicles the life and work of the Spanish singer Concha Piquer. Berrocal teaches workshops on comics and graphic novels in various institutions.

Mireia Pérez (b. 1984, Valencia) studied Fine Arts in Valencia, Madrid and Angoulême. She started her cartooning career working for the humorous weekly online magazine *El Estafador*, and has since worked as a graphic designer and illustrator and directed three short films. In 2010, she won the Fnac-Sins Entido

Graphic Novel Award for her comic *La muchacha salvaje*. She is quite active in the Spanish comics scene, annually organizing Madrid's independent comic festival, GRAF.

Max (b. 1956, Barcelona) has been writing and drawing comics since the early '80s. In 1995 he founded the avant-garde comics anthology *Nosotros somos los muertos* (NSLM), which ran until 2007. In addition to his comics, he is also known for his illustration work, including a variety of posters, record covers, children books and other illustrations. His graphic novel *Bardin the Superrealist* won Spain's National Comics Award in 2007. A documentary film about his life and work, *Drawing Max*, directed by Paco Mulet and himself, was an official selection of the 2021 FIFA (*Festival Intérnational du Film sur l'Art*) in Montréal. Since 2014, his satirical comic strip, *Trampantojo*, has appeared weekly in *Babelia*, the literary supplement of *El País*.

J. Michael Francis (b. Calgary, Alberta) is a Hough Family Endowed Chair and a Professor of History at the University of South Florida, St. Petersburg campus. Author of many publications, Francis also serves as the Executive Director of La Florida: The Interactive Digital Archive of the Americas (www.laflorida.org).

Eduardo Garrigues (b. Madrid) is an award-winning Spanish novelist and a diplomat. He is an honorary founding member of the Fundación Consejo España-EEUU and has written numerous essays related to the Spanish legacy in the United States. His historical novel *El que tenga valor que me siga* (2016) is focused on the figure of Bernardo de Gálvez.

James D. Fernández (b. New York) is a Professor of Spanish Literature and Culture at New York University. The grandson of Asturian immigrants, he has tried to reforge the links with Spain that were broken in his father's generation, because they didn't have the luxury to look back; they were too busy working, adapting, surviving.

Luis Argeo was born and raised in an Asturian town where the memories of emigration to the US were tucked away in attics and cluttered closets. A journalist and documentary filmmaker, he uses a camera and a microphone to record stories to help recover the traces of that emigration.

Fernández and Argeo are the co-curators of the exhibition *Invisible Immigrants: Spaniards in the US (1868–1945)*.

Lucía Cotarelo Esteban (b. Madrid) got her PhD in Spanish Literature at the Complutense University of Madrid (UCM). She is now a postdoctoral researcher at the Autonomous University of Barcelona. She is an expert on the literature and culture of the Spanish Republican exiles in the US.

Juan Pimentel (b. Madrid) is a writer and a science historian at the CSIC (Spanish National Research Council). He has been a visiting scholar at the University of Cambridge in the UK. His latest books are *The Rhinoceros and the Megatherium* (2017) and *Fantasmas de la ciencia española* (2020).

Estrella de Diego (b. Madrid) is an essayist, a Professor at UCM and full member of the Academia de Bellas Artes of San Fernando in Madrid. She was an invited Scholar for the Chair of Spanish Culture and Civilization (KJCC/NYU) and an invited Ida Cordelia Beam Distinguished Professorship (The University of Iowa). She is a member of the Board of Trustees of the Spanish Academy in Rome, the Prado Museum, the Cervantes Institute and the Norman Foster Foundation.

María Dolores Jiménez-Blanco (b. Granada) is a distinguished Spanish art historian and an expert on museums. She has been a member of the Board of Trustees of the Prado Museum since 2013. From 2018–2020, she was the Chair of the Department of Art History at the Complutense University of Madrid. In September 2020, she was appointed General Director of Bellas Artes by the Spanish Minister.

Ana Merino / Editor and curator (b. Madrid) is an award-winning writer and a Professor of Spanish Creative Writing and Cultural Studies at the University of Iowa. She has written extensive criticism on comics and graphic novels. She has authored two academic books and a monograph on Chris Ware and has curated five comic book exhibitions. She was a member of the ICAF (International Comic Arts Forum) Executive Committee from 2001–2011 and a Directors Board founder member at The Center for Cartoon Studies from 2004–2014.

Ernesto Coro / Project coordinator (b. Gijón) is the Director of Cultural Programs at the Cultural Office of the Embassy of Spain. He enjoys transforming and developing ideas into real projects. His passion for the arts has given him the opportunity to work in Spain, Australia, Scotland, Canada and the US. Trained in music and arts management, he hopes to finish his PhD one day.